INTRODUCING MEDIEVAL
ANIMAL NAMES

INTRODUCING MEDIEVAL
ANIMAL NAMES

BEN PARSONS

UNIVERSITY OF WALES PRESS

2025

www.uwp.co.uk
British Library CIP Data

A catalogue record for this book is available from the British Library
ISBN   978-1-83772-261-7
eISBN   978-1-83772-262-4

For GPSR enquiries please contact:
Easy Access System Europe OÜ, 16879218
Mustamäe tee 50, 10621, Tallinn, Estonia. *gpsr.requests@easproject.com*

MIX
Paper | Supporting responsible forestry
FSC
www.fsc.org   FSC® C013604

Designed and typeset by Chris Bell, cbdesign
Printed and bound by CPI Group (UK) Ltd, Croydon, CR0 4YY

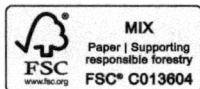

For Stan, Olly, Daisy, Ralph and Molly,
and all the other dogs I have known.
But most of all for Nina, *ubique verum
lux mei mundi.*

SERIES EDITORS' PREFACE

THE UNIVERSITY OF WALES PRESS series on Medieval Animals explores the historical and cultural impact of animals in this formative period, with the aim of developing new insights, analysing cultural, social and theological tensions and revealing their remarkable resonances with our contemporary world. The series investigates ideas about animals from the fifth century to the sixteenth, and from all over the world. Medieval thought on animals preserved and incorporated a rich classical and mythological inheritance, and some attitudes towards animals that we might consider as having characterized the Middle Ages persisted up to the Enlightenment era – and even to the present day.

CONTENTS

CHAPTER 1

ARE YOU THERE?
NAMING AND
ITS QUESTIONS

C

T HE QUESTION at the centre of this book is a relatively simple one. It asks what medieval people chose to call the animals they lived and worked with, surveying the proper names they assigned to their pets, livestock, working animals, and even the wild animals that surrounded them. Its intellectual ambitions are similarly uncomplicated: by exploring this topic, it hopes to lay bare an aspect of medieval culture that has to date received only sporadic attention, appearing as a tangential issue in studies of pet-keeping, popular culture or onomastics.[1] However, like many such questions, its simplicity is deceptive. Although the topic of animal-naming is straightforward, even trivial, it does not take a great deal of probing to see a whole constellation of other questions bound up with it. As soon as we start to think about what happens when we give an animal a name, let alone what choices are available for naming a non-human creature, multiple lines of enquiry open up.

A sense of these complexities can be grasped by looking to the period itself and its thoughts on appellation. Although animal names exercised some of the sharpest academic minds of the Middle Ages, from Isidore of Seville

C

to Peter Abelard, one of the most revealing meditations appears in E*stula*, a fabliau or short comic narrative from the first half of the thirteenth century. While mild by the genre's standards, the text exemplifies the comic potential that medieval people often saw in animals and their names. It was also relatively popular, occurring in three surviving manuscripts, and giving rise to analogous stories in other European languages.[2]

The story itself concerns two orphaned brothers to whom 'poverty was a dear friend' ('povretez fu bien lor amie').[3] Driven to dire straits, the brothers decide to mount a nocturnal raid on the vegetable-garden and sheep-pen of a wealthy *preudom*. One equips himself with a sack, the other with a knife and, after entering the yard, they split up to target the cabbage-patch and enclosure respectively. However, as one brother gropes about looking for the plumpest sheep, the *preudom* hears the commotion and orders his son to summon their dog; the boy does so, calling 'Estula, Estula'. Since the dog's name resembles the phrase 'es tu la?' ('are you there?'), when the brother in the pen hears him, he thinks his accomplice is calling and responds: 'Yes, for sure – I am here' ('Oïl voirement, sui je ci'). The boy then races back to his father, convinced that their dog has learned to speak. The father does not believe him, but promptly changes his mind when he too calls for Estula and receives the reply: 'truly I am here' ('voirement sui je çà'). Convinced that a great miracle has occurred, the father sends his son to fetch the local priest; after the priest protests that he cannot leave his house since he has no shoes, the son carries him on his back. When the brothers see the two of them in the dark, they mistake the priest's white vestments for a fleece, and the one with the knife orders his brother to throw this fat sheep to the ground so that he can slit its throat. Understandably, the priest panics and flees, leaving his clothing behind after it catches on a fencepost. The poor brothers do not only feed well on their stolen sheep and cabbage, but retrieve the discarded surplice the next morning and pawn it.

Beneath the playful knockabout, and the gleeful subversion of morality and poetic justice, there are serious lessons to be learned here. First and foremost, Estula makes clear that choosing a name for an animal is a significant decision. Not only is Estula's name sufficiently important to provide the focus for its story, but it determines the entire trajectory of the central joke. There can be no doubt that the father and son are set up as laughing stocks. They suffer the standard penalties of fabliau justice, through material loss on the one hand and humiliation on the other, and the poem explicitly invites the audience to mock them: the priest even tells the son at one point 'you are completely mad' ('tu es tout fol'). The main trigger for this derision is their dog's name: it is the unorthodoxy and ambiguity of this label that generates the confusion in the first place, and which leads to their display of foolish credulity and to their robbery and ridicule. In other words, the story shows that there are rules for naming animals, or at least broad norms, and that violating them might carry severe repercussions.

Yet while Estula's name is eccentric in some respects, it also lays bare some of the idiosyncrasies of animal-naming. One immediately obvious feature here is the functionality of the name. By taking the form of a question or directive, the name is more than purely descriptive; it is also what might

be called a performative utterance, acting on its object rather than simply denoting it.[4] 'Estula' is a command or a summons as much as a designation, not merely indicating its referent but actively manipulating him. In its choice of name, therefore, the fabliau ends up anticipating Bertrand Russell's comments when meditating on what a name might 'mean' to the dog that carries it: as Russell writes, 'to the dog, his name means: "either I shall be rewarded because I approach my master, or I shall be punished because I do not"'.[5] Much like Russell, E*stula* recognises that an animal's name is not the basis of its identity: it is a means of control above all, an exercise of power over its object.

Perhaps more interesting again is a further point the text makes clear. One of the central oddities of the story is the fact that Estula himself is absent from it. While his name gives the text its punchline, its major plot-point, and its title in two manuscripts, Estula the dog plays no part in its events – he only ever appears in the imagination of the characters. We are in fact informed that 'it was fortunate for the two brothers that he was not that night in the yard' ('Mès de tant lor avint il biens / Que la nuit n'ert mie en la cort'). The point that emerges, therefore, is that the name of the dog has greater weight than the creature to which it is attached. Estula the dog does not need to be present because Estula the name carries the effects that drive the story forward. This in turn flags up one of the key peculiarities of animal names, the fact that they are given to objects that are by their very nature unable to participate in language. As Roy Harris and Christopher Hutton remind us, while language might make a dog speakable, he cannot become an actor within it: unlike a human child acquiring his or her proper noun, 'Rover never learns to speak his own name, or learns about its use in his absence'.[6] An animal's name is therefore always a human construction projected on to the non-human world. It is an expression of human needs and meanings created for human beings to use with other human beings, and imposed on to a silent, passive entity whose actual presence is largely incidental.

All told, despite the facetious nature of E*stula*, the poem draws out many of the larger questions animal-naming poses. By underscoring that the given name of an animal is driven by convention, that it is designed to perform a concrete function, and that it is always at some level an index of human motivations and needs, E*stula* brings into view some of the critical implications of names. It also signals why they are interesting, in analytic terms, and what they might reveal about the social world that shaped them. In effect, E*stula* makes clear that names should be regarded as a sort of code in which the ambitions and attitudes of medieval people towards their animals were lodged. Being a means by which they sought to define the animal sphere according to their own wishes, and by which they impressed their own demands on to that sphere, they provide a lens through which their aspirations for this resource might be glimpsed. The fact that these statements are in turn governed by a set of implicit rules lends them even greater value, making them expressions not merely of marginal personal beliefs but of collective ideas, originating within the communities in which medieval people participated.[7]

These questions will be developed at greater length throughout this book. As a whole, it will provide an overview of the animal names (or zoonyms) from the period,

documenting surviving names and tracing the larger patterns into which they fall. While it focuses on western Europe in the Middle Ages, it will also look to parallels with cultures outside this place and time, both to sharpen our understanding of medieval practice and to identify larger trends in conceptions of the animal. Each of the four chapters will take a broadly thematic approach, interrogating a variable or set of variables that shaped the names thought fit for non-human creatures. We start on a practical footing, outlining the source materials in which extant names are preserved. Nonetheless, as will quickly become apparent, even this simple enquiry raises several larger issues; the very act of recording an animal's name proves highly loaded and densely layered. The remaining chapters explore these complexities further. The second looks to the classical background of medieval culture, comparing the naming customs of Greece and Rome to those of the Middle Ages. In the process, it again stirs up larger questions, asking what continuities are perceptible across the chronological divide, and why this might be. This is followed by a discussion of the uneasy relationship between species and naming. Although this book is not centrally concerned with taxonomies – 'naming' here will refer to the proper nouns given to individual creatures rather than generic species-labels – names can reveal much about the ways in which medieval language organised and schematised the natural world, as this chapter will demonstrate. Finally, we will consider one of the most commonly misunderstood aspects of medieval naming, its tendency to give human names (anthroponyms) to animals. As well as offering a corrective to current scholarly consensus, and showing how medieval habits remain embedded in our speech today, this chapter also reveals an important ethical point, showing how easily mechanisms used to disenfranchise animals can be turned against human beings.

But over and above these issues, there is also a further implication that will hover over this book. Once again, the events of E*stula* help bring this to light. One of the most striking features of Estula's name is its power to confuse. The misunderstanding that it produces is of course the entire point of the text, as the initial pronouncement of the dog's name acts as the first domino in a series of escalating errors. What is remarkable, however, is the nature of this confusion. Even at first glance, Estula represents a muddling of human and animal identities: when a summons for a dog causes one of the brothers to reply, it is momentarily unclear whether a human or canine has in fact responded, and chaos proceeds from there. This in turn draws out one of the chief peculiarities of zoonyms. By their very nature these labels represent a confusion of human and animal. Granting an animal a name makes it exceptional, separating it from the undifferentiated mass into which beasts are normally consigned. To echo David Herman, zoonyms challenge the sense that 'agential selfhood' does not reach 'beyond the human', acknowledging at some level that their referents are individuals worthy of recognition, if only as specimens or symbols; in short, a name proclaims that a particular creature merits discussion as a singular being.[8] Animal names are by their very nature transgressive, collapsing the venerable hierarchy that has been a mainstay of western thought since Aristotle.[9] But acknowledging this state of affairs only prompts further questions: when such

potential is implicit in these names, how did medieval culture prevent confusion from spreading, as it does in the world of E*stula*? How did it ensure that individualising an animal did not award it the same level of subjectivity as a human being? These issues will also resonate throughout the chapters that follow. We will think about the ways in which zoonyms maintain the division between human and animal, and how they balance the competing demands of specifying and generalising their object. In sum, we shall see how the peculiar properties of animal-naming stopped language from going entirely to the dogs.

CHAPTER 2

UNCOMMON NOUNS: HUNTING FOR ANIMAL NAMES

I N 1505 JEAN LEMAIRE DE BELGES composed *Les épîtres de l'amant vert* ('The Letters of the green lover'), two verse-epistles addressed to Margaret of Austria following the death of her second husband, Philibert II.[1] Lemaire's work took the popular form of the *consolatio*, a mode favoured by authors such as Machaut, Chaucer and Froissart when writing for a recently bereaved patron; less conventionally, at least until his poem created a micro-genre in its wake, Jean delivered his consoling message through the persona of Margaret's dead pet parrot.[2] In the course of the poem, Jean makes the bird offer many routine assurances to Margaret. He emphasises the greater joys found after death, and the continuity of earthly ties beyond the grave, before concluding with a lavish statement of his enduring affection for his mistress. However, the most extraordinary sequence in this eminently strange poem comes in its second part. Here the parrot is received into a kind of zoological paradise populated by 'a thousand noble birds and creatures' ('de mille oiseaux et d'animaulx gentilz'). The residents of this plane are reported at length, and constitute a veritable who's who of notable animals from ancient and medieval literature:

Among and amidst them, there trots and walks
The sparrow of Catullus' friend
Who, when Death wickedly seized her,
Was mourned in noble verse ...
Also there is the pair of turtledoves
That were offered, according to the custom,
When Jesus received his circumcision;
And the good cockerel that reminded St Peter
Of his misdeed, the great loss and the price he paid;
And the dove of innocent wisdom
Who returned with the olive branch;
An eagle, the powerful emblem of Charlemagne,
Flying high; and the swan of Cleves;
The porcupine, the glory of Orleans;
And the very splendid ermine of Brittany.
And besides, above the sweet flowers,
Go fluttering the bees and little flies
Who visited Plato, while he slept in his cradle.[3]

The narrative continues in this vein for a further sixty lines. Other honoured creatures in this whistle-stop tour include: the housefly for whom Virgil held a funeral; the donkey Mary rode to Bethlehem; the ox at the manger; the sheep who provided Jason's golden fleece; the bear of St Vaast and the pig of St Anthony; the dog that cleaned St Roc's sores; the porpoise that rescued Arion; St Jerome's lion, St George's horse, St Margaret's lambs, and many more besides. The vision wraps up by emphasising the lack of discord among this host of creatures, before noting that the list could be extended still further: 'There were more again without number, / That I cannot calculate and cannot count' ('Même encor plus sans nombre, / Que je ne compte et que je ne dénombre').

This passage is remarkable for a number of reasons, and not merely for its mildly heretical vision of an afterlife for illustrious beasts. In the first place, it provides emphatic testimony to the depth at which animals were embedded in the various iconographic languages of the Middle Ages. In compiling this catalogue, Lemaire's focus ranges over several discourses, from historiography and heraldry to classical poetry and hagiography. But what is most striking here is the absence of names from this list. Even though the poem is a work of commemorative mourning, and deals with exceptional creatures, almost all are pictured in terms of their species and achievements alone. There are in fact only three named organisms in a list of over three dozen – Alexander's horse Bucephalus, another horse named Montaigue, and the greyhound Brutus – but beyond these instances proper nouns play no role in Lemaire's fantasy. It is not even clear how we should read the term by which Lemaire refers to his parrot-narrator: 'l'amant vert' could conceivably be either an appellative or descriptive epithet. In short, naming is clearly not an important part of Lemaire's tribute to the capabilities of animals. Although he can assemble an extensive roll-call of animals from multiple literary traditions, there is no comparable tradition of naming for him to utilise.

This reticence is not peculiar to Lemaire. His work encapsulates one of the most puzzling features of animal-naming in the Middle Ages, the fact that the period contains relatively few recorded names. Despite the wide range of material and symbolic uses to which medieval people put

animals, and the wealth of archaeological, literary and documentary evidence showing their reliance on them, names
prove surprisingly elusive: although a sizeable corpus can be
pieced together, when set against the profusion of reference
to animals of all kinds, they are a comparative rarity. It is
not difficult to find other authors withholding the names of
even noteworthy creatures. In medieval historiography, for
instance, Suger gives no name to the 'devil of a pig' who
caused Philip of France to be fatally thrown from his horse in
1131, just as John Trevisa does not name the cat who inspired
an Oxford scribe to declare himself 'heire of Englond' in
1316, or Roger of Wendover the wolf that guarded Edmund
of East Anglia's head after his murder in 869; while all three
marvel at the remarkable actions of these animals, none
attribute personal names to them.[4] In religious as well as
secular history the same pattern holds true. Although multiple saints are associated with beasts, there is no tradition of
giving names to these symbolic companions. In Jacobus de
Voragine's great thirteenth-century compendium of *vitae*, no
names are allocated to the she-bear Mamertinus frees from
a trap, the lion that helps Zozimus dig a grave, or the pet
cat whose friendship with a hermit earns Gregory's scorn.[5]
Perhaps the closest is an anecdote Brunforte tells of Francis
of Assisi in *c*.1300, in which the saint calms a man-eating
wolf by addressing him as 'Frate Lupo' ('Brother Wolf'), but
even here the creature's 'name' is merely a statement of its
species rather than a personal marker.[6]

Of course, there might be any number of reasons for
leaving these beasts anonymous: it would make greater
sense to imply that they were embodiments of divine or
diabolical will than present them as agencies in their own

right. However, the silence grows all the more surprising when we turn to contexts where we might expect to see names, especially those that award animals some level of personhood. This is especially true of the literature of the period, which dedicates entire genres to giving animals voices, although without showing any obligation to name them. Typical is the Middle English bird-debate. In the earliest example of the form, the *Owl and the Nightingale* (*c*.1272), the two title-characters trade such insults as 'galegale' ('chatterer') and 'wrecche þing' ('wretched thing') but never refer to one another by name.[7] The same holds in later debates: from the *Thrush and the Nightingale* (*c*.1300) and *Cuckoo and the Nightingale* (*c*.1380) up to David Lyndsay's *Complaynt of our Soverane Lordis Papyngo* (*c*.1530), bird-speakers invariably go unnamed. Occasionally a text might preserve a generic folk-name – a debate composed in *c*.1400 introduces the 'rusti chateryng of þe iay' with the colloquial term 'watte' – but the transformation of birds into speaking subjects does not usually involve naming them.[8] Much the same state of affairs is found in the beast-fable. Aside from the major exception of *Ysengrimus* (*c*.1149) and the later stories of Reynard the Fox, in which the 'names and personalities' of animal-characters are a vital element, most examples are content to identify their actors simply as 'the hare', 'the flea', 'the ass' or 'the peacock'.[9]

Still more startling is the macabre ritual of the animal trial, in which livestock were tried and executed, normally for mauling children. The documents preserving these strange events sometimes describe the condemned in some detail, but generally stop short of recording their names. Hence a hangmen's receipt from Falaise in 1386, which details the execution of a pig guilty of mutilating a child's face, merely pictures the accused as 'a sow aged three years or thereabouts' ('une truie de l'age de 3 ans ou environ'); a similar account from Beaupré, regarding the execution of a bull in 1499 who had gored a teenage boy to death, simply identifies the creature as a 'bull with red hair' ('thorreau de poil rouge').[10] One anomaly is Verray, a pig hanged at Arnay-le-Duc in 1444 for killing a young girl; but even this label seems to record the animal's species rather than being a proper noun, since it is likely a form of *verres* ('domesticated boar').[11] Although these documents afford creatures sufficient humanness to prosecute them under human law, 'interpellating these beasts … with legal personhood', they stop short of granting them humanlike names.[12]

Artefacts relating to animal-keeping tell the same story. Although numerous collars survive from the period, and more yet appear in visual and literary sources, they tend to share the same blind spot. It is true that most surviving examples are purely functional objects: the bulk are simply spiked chain-link devices designed to protect the vulnerable throats of hounds, such as the pieces in the Hunt collection at Leeds Castle.[13] Yet even when they take decorative form, they are more likely to reflect the identity of an owner or the fact of ownership than the name of their wearer. In the hunt-scene depicted in the famous Unicorn Tapestries (*c*.1500), for instance, two greyhounds sport collars embroidered with the monogram AE, likely a coded reference to the tapestry's commissioners; the coat of arms Jean Fouquet painted for Simon de Varie in 1455 likewise incorporates a greyhound supporter whose collar is inscribed with an anagram of Varie's name, 'Vie A Mon Desir' ('Life After My

Desire').[14] The collar of the 'spotless deer' ('candida cerva') in Petrarch's Sonnet 190, and of the hind in Thomas Wyatt's English reworking, follow the same course; in either case, the message 'written her fair neck round about' merely concerns the deer's subjection to Caesar.[15] Once again, zoonyms fail to turn up where we might expect them.

In short, despite the quantity of beasts that run, fly and slither through the medieval records – records that are themselves inscribed on their skins with styli made from their feathers – the vast majority remain unnamed.[16] Anonymity is the norm, even when the distance between human and animal is closed. What is more, this habit seems to be peculiar to the western Middle Ages. Neighbouring cultures in both space and time developed complex traditions of naming around exactly the sort of creature medieval sources pass over. As we shall see in following chapters, classical mythographers paid extensive attention to the names of non-human beings, from Actaeon's hunting-pack to Augeas' cattle. In Islam, the *aḥādīth* place several named animals in Muhammad's possession, including the mule Duldul (Porcupine), the camel al-Qaswa (Split-ears), the donkey Ufair (Gazelle), and the horses al-Mandub (Approved) and al-Murtajiz (Impulsive).[17] Buddhism likewise takes care to name Nālāgiri, the mad elephant sent to trample Buddha by his envious cousin Devadatta; Norse mythology also attaches a long list of names to horses, hawks, pigs, wolves and other animals, even awarding a name to Ratatoskr (Awl-toothed), the impudent squirrel who inhabits the world-tree Yggdrasil.[18] While it is going too far to infer an active taboo in medieval Christian culture, the period is unusually content to ignore or suppress its zoonyms.

However, this reserve is not merely a stumbling-block, but a valuable question in its own right; the silence of the records is an eloquent one. It reveals two points of particular interest, confirming what is at stake in animal-naming, and hinting at some of the mechanics by which it operated. The main impression to emerge is that a proper noun is not required when individualising an animal. The general willingness of the sources to dispense with names even as they allocate beasts significance or subjectivity makes clear that designations are superfluous to these processes. Needless to say, this is very different from the ways in which human beings are defined: as Saul Kripke reminds us, naming is a fundamental component in creating the human subject, since the entire purpose of an anthroponym is to function as a 'rigid designator' by which 'other speakers in the community' can recognise the uniqueness of its bearer.[19] In fact, if we follow the psychoanalyst Jacques Lacan, then a human name can be seen as the lynchpin of social identity, forcing entry into the dense network of obligations and relationships Lacan calls the Symbolic Order, in which 'the subject' is 'inscribed at birth, if only by virtue of his proper name'.[20] What is more, medieval linguistic theory thoroughly understood these connections between language and selfhood, as Corey Marvin has shown.[21] When we move to animal-naming, however, this same rigidity begins to loosen. In other words, we start to see language behaving in distinct ways across the species boundary, as naming sheds its association with identity on the animal side of the divide.

What gives these concerns added weight is that they link up with one of the major preoccupations of the relatively new discipline of animal studies. Not only has this field stressed the importance of studying earlier cultures when assessing our own ideas of the animal, but the behaviour of language has emerged as a central strand within it.[22] Such a focus is already detectible in the earliest inroads into these debates. As far back as the early nineteenth century, the philosopher Jeremy Bentham noted a similar slipperiness around the semantics of animal names. Reflecting on the word 'puss', Bentham observed its potential to fluctuate between generic and specific: he notes that 'puss' is at once broad and particular in its meaning, a summons 'applied to the purpose of feeding several cats' on the one hand, and on the other 'to each respective cat … a proper name'.[23] However, this thinking has received its most influential formulation in the final lectures of Jacques Derrida. Building on Bentham's reflections, Derrida asserts that 'the animal' can only be understood in light of speech and the definitions it confers, being at root 'a word that men have given themselves to give'; in other words, it is language that has allowed human beings to differentiate themselves from all other organisms, and to privilege those who can speak over those who cannot.[24] As we shall see in due course, the ethical and ethnographic inflection of Derrida's work, and its development by later writers such as Wolfe and Senior, picks out an important current running through medieval naming-systems, where the choice of names often meshes with the treatment of other marginalised beings.[25]

But alongside these theoretical considerations, the caginess of medieval texts also signals how they ought to be approached. Since the sources are usually content to leave even prominent animals unnamed, the appearance of a zoonym clearly represents a deliberate choice, a point at which an author has opted to break the customary silence. The case is much as Jane Bliss presents it in her discussion of dogs and weapons in medieval romance: as Bliss suggests, a text automatically makes itself 'different in feel' when it chooses to give a title to an animal or object 'because nobody expects them to be named'.[26] To put this another way, the recording of a name is itself a charged, even calculated gesture; it suggests that the creature or name has some form of significance for the text in which it is cited. The very appearance of a creature's name in writing is a marker of that creature's value in the eyes of the text, declaring that an author, audience or discourse has seen some special quality or worth in it. Naming, simply put, is inseparable from evaluation.

Taking this point further, when we turn to the extant names themselves, it is possible to see three types of value determining their survival. The most conspicuous and perhaps most predictable is monetary value: in blunt terms, there is a direct correlation between a creature's price-tag and its likelihood to be named. It is for this reason that we know the names of Gibbun (Hunchback), Blakemanne (Blackman), and the other gyrfalcons and hawks owned by Henry III and his father John: these valuable creatures appear in the closed rolls alongside detailed instructions for their care and exercise, such as a note in March 1215 ordering John Fitz Hugh to feed Gibbun 'fat goats' ('pingues capras') and 'good chickens' ('bonas gallinas'), or the regimen mandated for Blakemanne in October 1219.[27] The same factor underpins one of the richest sources for English horse-names, the list of gifts given by Edward the Black Prince in 1352.[28] Again, the preservation of these equestrian names is a direct result of the high value of the organisms, both as tokens of royal favour and products of considerable investment: writing in *c.*1332, William of Pagula estimates that 'one great horse' would run up the same weekly expenses as 'four or five paupers'.[29] In fact. in a few sources, we can even see financial concerns working in a conspicuously selective way, picking out which animals are named and which are passed over. In a property dispute heard at the Chartreuse de Vallon in 1360, the name of the horse Moreta is specified, but those of two cows, three sheep and two goats are not.[30] The 1515 will Robert Wilkynson, vicar of Northfrothingham, toes the same line: Wilkynson names his three horses Gryme, Brun and Sorell Gosell, but not the two 'oxen of the best' noted alongside them.[31] A further instance is the 1358 will of Thomas de la Mare of York, where proper nouns are allocated to all items of high monetary value: alongside his three horses Turnebull, Bayard de Wirethorp and Morell de Welwik, Thomas also lists Hyngler, a 'small knife' ('cultellum') in his possession.[32]

However, financial value is not the only determinant that can be seen in the texts. Perhaps more appealing is the emotional esteem that hovers behind many citations. While it would be a mistake to project modern sensibilities on to medieval people, as work on the history of emotions has amply demonstrated, some evidence can hardly be interpreted any other way.[33] Many names speak for themselves, such as Chier (Dear), the dog for whom Louis XI commissioned an elaborate collar from the goldsmith Jacques de Chefdeville in 1463.[34] Equally emphatic is the appearance of named pets on funerary monuments. Examples include Iakke, a dog on the 1448 memorial brass of Sir Brian de Stapleton and his wife Cecilia, or Parceval and Dyamant, two greyhounds that form part of the 1391 effigy of Sir Jehan de Seure in Ozouer-le-Repos.[35] The owners' desire to commemorate these three dogs on their own personal memorials, in places normally reserved for children and spouses, clearly points to exceptional fondness for them. The same is true of an odd tribute composed in *c.*1530 by the owner of the 'fox whelpe' Curribus (Chariots), after his neighbours had killed it 'with staffe, clubbe and flayle'. The account of this 'gentle' beast, who was 'more merueylous' and 'craftyer to watche' than any 'catte', gives no reason to doubt that it is the heartfelt, grief-stricken tribute it purports to be.[36] Occasionally names appear in even more lavish acts of memorialisation. An extreme case is al-Yahshur, prized hawk of Murshid ibn Munqidh in the early 1120s, whose remarkable loyalty earned an extravagant funeral procession from Mahmud ibn Qaraja, lord of Hama.[37] As we shall see in later chapters, affection is not the sole emotion that might cause an animal's name to be preserved, but it remains a powerful stimulus.

A larger and more pervasive motivation, however, is what might be called rhetorical value. In many cases, names obviously fulfil some symbolic function for their texts. Sometimes they achieve this by their sheer banality. Hence the everyday names for creatures found in proverbs and other snippets of popular wisdom serve to ground the texts in lived experience. Two key examples are the French saying 'qui Fauvel sevent torcher' and its English equivalent 'cury Favel', first attested in 1319 and *c.*1420, respectively, which are both built around customary names for a horse or ass; the fifteenth-century proverbs 'loke ye bete not Bayard' and 'blynd Bayard of no dowtys doth purvey' likewise call on another widespread name for a drayhorse.[38] Similar names also appear in teaching texts, often performing the time-honoured strategy of bringing unfamiliar information into line with the world of the pupil.[39] In a set of classroom exercises from 1519, the Oxford schoolmaster John Stanbridge alludes to a traditional name for a pet or performing monkey, suggesting that 'Simea os distorquet' ('the ape contorts its mouth') might be rendered 'Iacke napes maketh a mowe'.[40] In 1530 John Palsgrave quotes two standard names for a mare in his English-French dictionary: among his indispensable phrases are 'What! gyppe, Gyll with a galde backe ... hey! de par le diable, Gilotte'.[41]

However, on top of these relatively simple functions, names can also be used to generate more complex meanings. Not infrequently, they serve a comic purpose, deflating an elevated discourse by injecting a note of mundane bestialism into it. An archetypal example is the pursuit of the fox through the farmyard in Chaucer's *Nun's Priest's Tale* (*c*.1390), which burlesques Ovid's story of Actaeon and John Gower's *Visio Anglie* (1381) in one fell swoop, and works by displacing Ovid's Latinised Greek terms with the homelier dog-names Colle, Talbot and Gerland.[42] A similar process is at work in Leon Battista Alberti's parody of classical funeral inscriptions, which inserts the dog Canis and his sire Megastomo (Bigmouth) into a pompous recital of this 'most ancient family' who served 'in the households of countless most illustrious princes'.[43] Also comparable is the sequence of Welsh names in the story of Culhwch from the *Mabinogion* (*c*.1250), a list that includes the boars Ysgithyrwyn (White-tusk) and Twrch Trwyth (Boar-chief), the dogs Call

(Clever) and Cuall (Stupid), and the horses Hwyrddyddwg (Slow-carrier) and Drwddyddwg (Woe-carrier).[44] Given the text's bewildering proliferation of titles and quests, which includes an inventory of several hundred heroes and almost forty trials, these names compound the overall sense of absurdist exaggeration. But the worldliness of zoonyms can also have more sophisticated, non-comic functions too. In the play the *Killing of Abel*, performed at Wakefield in the fifteenth century as part of the town's annual Corpus Christi cycle, the oxen that pull Cain's plough are listed as Greynhorne, Gryme, Donnyng, Mall, Stott, Lemyng, Morell and Whitehorne. These quotidian English names are clearly part of the cycle's wider policy of restaging biblical history in the here and now, in order to emphasise its eternity and universality.[45] Despite their various implications, in short, what unites all these names is that they have entered the written record in order to trigger certain meanings. Again, we can glimpse a sort of filtration process at work beneath the textual evidence, determining which animals are named and which are not, in this case choosing names according to the connotations that they carry.

While these concerns will be teased out at greater length in subsequent chapters, they already allow a couple of rough conclusions to be formed. In the first place, they make clear that names give direct insight into the qualities medieval people found desirable in their animals. Even before we consider the literal meaning of a given name, its very appearance in the record already represents a judgement, a sense that its referent has measured up to a standard or answered a requirement. However, it is also possible to draw a further point from this. The fact that the documents are restricted to valuable animals – whether they be valuable in a pecuniary, emotional or rhetorical sense – shows the extent to which utility governs medieval views of the animal. The records confirm Pieter Beullens' point that use-value dominates conceptions of animals in the Latin west: recording a proper noun is much like the material usages Beullens outlines, treating the named creature as the literary equivalent of 'food for the hungry, game for the huntsmen … personal aids for the labourer or the traveller'.[46] In other words, even when they are individualised, or allowed to enter language with much the same standing as human beings, animals are still resources to be exploited.

However, the patchiness of the records also has implications for reading and discussing them in practical terms. Since names appear sporadically, they can only be meaningfully surveyed by casting a wide net. It is true that a few individual sources contain large caches of names: two especially valuable examples are the catalogue of horses in the *Chanson de Roland* (*c.*1115), and the eighty dogs entered into a fund-raising lottery at Zurich in 1504, apparently to maximise their owners' chances of winning.[47] But these are isolated cases, and by and large the evidence is scattered. Consequently, a corpus of names must be stitched together from a wide variety of hints and traces. The following pages will therefore bring together animals from a range of different media: from documents such as wills, household inventories, accounts and correspondence; from pictorial sources such as inscriptions and manuscript illuminations; from artefacts such as seals, medallions and heraldic devices; from fleeting mentions in historiography, mythography and

philosophy. As will quickly become apparent, although animal names cannot be found everywhere, they can be found more or less anywhere.

While this wide-ranging, bird's-eye approach is prompted by the records, a few of the materials considered here deserve further comment. One of the first points to acknowledge is the role of literary discourse in this enquiry. The period's imaginative writing has proven the most vital resource in locating named animals, especially its poetry and drama. Of course, the fictive nature of these texts means they cannot be taken at face value, as straightforward representations of animals or their names. Some of their names self-evidently do not mirror general practice and make little claim to do so. This is most obvious in the case of overtly allegorical names, which treat their bearers as metaphors rather than proxies for actual creatures. Hence, Huginn ('Thought') and Muninn ('Memory'), Oðinn's two raven-spies in the *Grímnismál* (*c*.950), obviously serve to signify their owner's knowledge rather than any real-world convention.[48] Similarly removed from reality are the hounds Harre ('Diligence'), Wunne ('Pleasure') and Triuwe ('Loyalty') in Hadamar von Laber's complex love-allegory *Die Jagd* (*c*.1330).[49] Wilfully grotesque or outlandish names present similar problems, such as Croacus (Croaker) and Rodilardus (Fat-Chomper), kings of the frogs and mice in Elisius Calentius' translation of the *Batrachomyomachia* (1534).[50] Both can be discounted as 'authentic' names owing to their pointedly bizarre forms and application to species beyond the limits of domestication.

Yet despite these outliers, it does not take a great deal of scrutiny to show that the line between literary and concrete practice is a hazy one. Most names in fictional narrative can usually be accepted as fair representatives of actual naming practice, since they often hinge on the reader recognising them as typical for a certain species or class. Thus, when the eponymous hero of the romance *Ipomadon* (c.1390) disguises himself as a lunatic by dressing in a 'thredbare tabard' and mounting a horse named Gylle, causing hilarity within the court, the joke only makes sense if the name is seen as an accepted designation for a working or draft mare.[51] The same is true of Peter Abelard's satirical syllogism of c.1120, which ridicules the philosophical school of realism by 'proving' that Socrates and Brunellus are the same entity, and turns on the fact that Brunellus is a stereotypical name for a donkey.[52] Cases such as these are relatively commonplace, and remind us of Paul Strohm's dictum that even the most avowedly fictional texts are 'composed within history – if not within a sense of what did happen, at least within a sense of what might have happened, or what could be imagined'.[53] Although they describe imaginary animals, they nonetheless draw on existing ideas about what constitutes an appropriate label for a beast or type of beast. Indeed, when seen in these terms, even the most outrageous names can be revealing: by flagrantly violating the implicit rules of naming, they bring its underlying grammar to light.

Another set of sources presents a different sort of challenge. Many key witnesses date from beyond the conventional frontiers of the Middle Ages, having been composed in the sixteenth and sometimes seventeenth centuries. While we might be accustomed to seeing a radical rupture between the medieval and modern periods, the information provided by these sources is frequently invaluable. In part

this is due to early modern lexicographers deliberately con-
serving traditional names as part of their larger projects.
However, later texts can be just as vital when operating less
self-consciously, since they often contain stray references
that allow longer traditions to be traced. Two cases in point
are the venerable but spottily attested cat-names Puss and
Malkin. The first glimpse of Puss appears in 1256, where it
appears in the name of a Northumberland murder victim: in
a textbook case of adding insult to injury, an assize roll for
this year notes that 'Ilyf le Messer wounded Robert Pussycat
[Robertus Pussekat] by the bridge of Corbridge from which
injury he immediately died'.[54] Although it can be inferred
that the word was already a common cat-name at this
point, or at least sufficiently well-established to be used as
a nickname, we have to wait until the sixteenth century to
find it applied directly to felines: in *c.*1521 Skelton's *Speke
Parrot* compares its protagonist to a 'pus cat', and in 1533
'Pus my cat' is a pet in Heywood's play *Iohan Iohan*.[55] Malkin
likewise can only be reverse-engineered from early modern
sources. The name, a pet-form of Maud or Matilda, does not
appear as a zoonym until William Baldwin's proto-gothic
satire *Beware the Cat* (*c.*1553), where Grimmalkin is the ruler
of a secret underworld of cats.[56] However, Baldwin seems to
be using an existing term in an extended sense: the compound form he employs is an elaborate piece of wordplay,
one which builds a nexus of sinister connotations around
cats, especially in the alternative spelling 'Grimolochin'
(i.e., Grim-idol). The name seems to have reverted back to
its original form after Baldwin's influence receded. While it
retains supernatural implications in *Macbeth* (*c.*1605) and
Middleton's *Witch* (*c.*1615), where Graymalkin and Malkin

are attendant demons, it has more neutral value later on: in an eighteenth-century translation of Reynard, Malkin is simply the name of the cat antagonist, and in Grose's dictionary of Regency slang 'Malkin, or Maulkin' is 'a general name for a cat'.[57] All in all, these sources show that modern material sometimes casts medieval evidence in a new light, enabling scattered dots of information to be joined into cohesive traditions.

Equally important are a number of post-medieval events that throw pet-naming into particularly stark relief. A major instance here is the English witch-panic of the Tudor and Stuart periods. Owing to the belief that witches were inevitably accompanied by a 'familiar spirit' in animal-form, the pets of the accused received an unusual level of scrutiny from prosecutors: as Helen Parish estimates, around 75 per cent of trials make reference to such creatures.[58] Although figures such as the self-appointed 'Witch-finder General' Matthew Hopkins might have claimed that these 'Imps names' were of a kind 'which no mortall could invent', the vast bulk are manifestly traditional.[59] Hence in his handbook for magistrates, the Puritan minister Richard Bernard vacillates between the extravagant and everyday when cataloguing familiars known to him:

> To these they give names; such as I have read of are these: *Mephastophilus*, *Lucifer*, *Little Lord*, *Fimodes*, *David*, *Inde*, *Little Robin*, *Smacke*, *Lightfoote*, *Non-such*, *Lunch*, *Makeshift*, *Swart*, *Pluck*, *Blue*, *Catch*, *White*, *Callico*, *Hard name*, *Tibb*, *Hiff*, *Ball*, *Puss*, *Rutterkin*, *Dick*, *Prettie*, *Griffet* and *Jacke*. And they meet together to Christen the spirits (as they speake) when they give the spirit a name.[60]

Despite opening with two impressively diabolical names, most of the appellations Bernard collects are longstanding designations for pets or working animals: variants of Robin, White, Lightfoote, Tibb, Ball, Dick and Jacke will all be found in subsequent chapters. Those with no documented history are still likely customary. Rutterkin is no doubt taken from the 1618 confession of Phillipa and Margaret Flower, which claims that the women's mother used a cat by this name to bewitch the children of the Earl of Rutland; however, the name later appears in an anecdote told of Henrietta Maria's dwarf Jeffrey Hudson, where Rutterkin is a cat whose skin Hudson wore in a prank that caused 'greatest Confusion and Clamour'.[61] Beyond Bernard's work, other witch pamphlets show similar patterns. For instance, in the 1572 confession of Elizabeth Stile, we find the equally well-established appellatives Bunn, Jyll and Jynne given to two cats and a 'kitling' allegedly fed on Stile's blood.[62] In fact, even the most fevered coinages of prosecutors often have at least one foot in reality. Among the menagerie of familiars reported by Hopkins in 1647 is 'Griezzell Greedigutt', whose name combines two much older titles: the first is a common descriptive name for a grey animal, first testified in 1303 among the horses of Richard of Gravesend, Bishop of London; the second is a standard dog-name found in Arthur Golding's 1567 version of Ovid's *Metamorphoses*, among other sources.[63] The point is that events like these, in which the status of animals and their bonds with human beings become momentarily fraught, cause the searchlight to shine particularly brightly on animal-naming.[64] They perform on a larger scale what the more disparate references also achieve, signalling when particular names were sufficiently pervasive to stretch beyond the fringes of the Middle Ages.

As a final point, this feature of naming underscores another significant aspect of zoonyms themselves, and why they repay attention. The very fact that it is possible to trace lines of continuity that pass clean through the divide between medieval and modern shows how artificial this division proves in practice, and the extent to which it is based in critical expediency rather than reality. When dealing with conventions such as these, which belong to a demotic level of culture beneath the dramatic sea-changes of scholarly discourse and royal politics, a greater degree of stability is only to be expected. After all, the treatment of animals and the attitudes, valuations and usages they attracted are likely to have remained relatively unchanged into the modern period, at least until the upheavals in agricultural practice at the close of the eighteenth century. Animal-naming does not just tell us about the ways in which medieval culture confronted the natural world, in effect, but exposes the striations within that culture itself. It reminds us that cultural transitions cannot be assumed to take place at every level of a particular society, but that any line drawn between periods can only ever be a jagged and approximate one. Indeed, this point will become only more obvious in our next chapter, which considers the opposing border, and compares medieval naming to the customs of the ancient world.

CHAPTER 3

FORMER ADDRESS:
NAMING BEFORE
THE MIDDLE AGES

WHATEVER ANIMAL NAMES might tell us about the past, in the ancient world they could occasionally predict the future. Cicero reports that just such a name inspired the Roman general Aemilius Paullus to victory before the battle of Pydna in 168 BCE. After hearing that his daughter's puppy Persa (Persian) had died, Paullus knew that he would go on to defeat the similarly named King Perseus of Macedon: he responded to the news by embracing his daughter and declaring 'I accept, my child, the portent' ('accipio … mea filia, omen').[1] A century and a half later, a comparable story is linked to Octavian, the future Emperor Augustus. As Suetonius records, Octavian received a similar omen before the battle of Actium in 31 BCE: on his way to the engagement, he met an ass called Nicon (Triumph) being driven by a man named Eutychus (Good Fortune). Once his fleet had crushed the combined forces of Cleopatra and Mark Anthony, the commander built a temple near the battle-site and placed inside bronze statues of both man and ass, such was his gratitude for this auspicious sign.[2]

These episodes, with their weird blurring of temporal barriers, highlight the importance of looking backwards

when trying to understand medieval conventions. At their simplest level, they remind us that animal names existed long before the Middle Ages, and that fixing appellatives to individual animals was not a medieval innovation, any more than keeping them as pets, mounts or beasts of burden. Indeed, given medieval literate culture's general reliance on classical models, it is only to be expected that its conceptualisation of animals would be indebted to earlier thinking; in their own way, these earlier names do point to the future, if not quite in the way that Augustus and Paullus assumed. However, the quintessential Romanness of these episodes, based as they are on a pagan preoccupation with signs and prodigies, also underscores a further point.[3] It emphasises that animal names can only take shape in the prevailing values of their given culture, and within its dominant conceptions of the natural world. As a result, antiquity can also provide a sort of limit case to medieval habits, a point of comparison that allows idiosyncrasies to stand out all the more starkly. This chapter will then see what can be learned from this earlier history, not merely as a prelude to the Middle Ages but as a phase of naming with its own peculiarities.

The history of animal-naming probably begins with the process of domestication itself. It is likely that simple calling-names or rough descriptives emerged when human beings first began to use animals in hunting and husbandry at the tail-end of the Younger Dryas (12900 BP), during the series of agricultural and environmental changes that mark the start of the Holocene epoch.[4] Nonetheless, for the first verifiable names, we have to look to the Egyptians. The earliest surviving zoonym seems to be that of

Abuwtiyuw, guard-dog of an unknown pharaoh of the Sixth Dynasty (2345–2181 BCE). Abuwtiyuw's memorial inscription survives at the mastaba cemetery near Giza, and records his burial with linen, incense and balms 'for the honour of Anubis'.[5] He is followed by a number of royal dogs in later funerary inscriptions: Tekal and Beha, two hunting hounds of Wahankh Intef II (2112–2063 BCE), depicted on a stele at El-Tarif; Satekai, Xabesu, Menmaufnahsi, Xafmes, Akena and Temaa from Dynasty XII (1991–1802 BCE); and Aya from *c.*1640 BCE, whose unnamed mistress interred him in a wooden coffin with a dedication to Osiris.[6] From the New Kingdom comes an unusual artefact, a pink leather collar decorated with the name Tantanuit and deposited in the tomb of Thutmose IV (*c.*1400–*c.*1390 BCE).[7] Alongside these relatively affectionate relics, other names appear in a more martial context. Several equestrian names occur among the temple reliefs celebrating the campaigns of Seti I (*c.*1290–1279 BCE) and his successor Ramesses II (1279–1213 BCE). At Karnak, horses drawing Seti's chariot are labelled Amon-As-signs-to-Him-the-Victory, Victory-in-Thebes, Great-in-Victory and Smiter-of-Foreigners; likewise, at Abu Simbel and other sites, Ramesses' horses at the battle of Kadesh bear the names Mut-is-Satisfied and Usermare-Setepnere-Beloved-of-Amon.[8] The Kadesh reliefs also preserve another canine name: a hound depicted in the act of savaging a Libyan captive is identified as Anath-is-Protection.[9]

While these names are interesting in several respects, not least for the mere fact of their survival, they also act as a potent restatement of many of the key questions around zoonyms. If anything, they present many of the factors we encountered in the last chapter in even more amplified form.

Most obviously, they show once again that the recording of a name is a mark of privilege, a momentary suspension of general silence. These isolated witnesses, distributed across a full millennium, obviously do not represent the total number of horses, dogs, cats, baboons or crocodiles with which Egyptians interacted: they are animals invested with an unusual level of merit, whose names are recorded as a direct result of that merit.[10] But these names also serve as a reminder that every zoonym is itself a complex package of judgements, and that the very allocation of a name involves assessing its bearer's usefulness to human beings. It is certainly telling that the records focus so heavily on dogs and horses, the two animals most deeply intertwined with human activity. Utility also registers in the names themselves. Beha is likely derived from 'behkai' (antelope), referring to the dog's speed, while Aya and the central syllables of Abuwtiyuw are probably onomatopoeic, imitating the barking required of them as hunters or watchdogs.[11] But at the same time, there is also an important signal in these Egyptian records that usefulness is itself a highly localised concept; what one community or group might deem useful may not necessarily be shared with others. Hence the memorials also preserve the name of the cats Tamyt (She-Cat) and Nojem (Sweet-natured), the former belonging to Prince Djhutmose (fourteenth century BCE), priest of Ptah, and the latter to Puyemrê (fifteenth century BCE), architect and priest of Amun.[12] Given the well-known veneration of cats in Egypt and the large number of surviving feline mummies, especially at the cult-centre of Bubastis, it would be strange if no cat-names had survived.[13] But their preservation underscores that the recording of a name is tied directly to the priorities of a given culture, priorities that may or may not extend beyond its bounds.

These features, and several others, become even more conspicuous when we turn to Greece and Rome. Here the record thickens considerably. Not only is there a higher volume of names spread across a greater range of texts and artefacts, but the period shows fuller self-awareness over naming: at times it draws up catalogues of names, such as the lists compiled by Xenophon, Arrian and Columella, and at others offers scholarly discussion of them. The sources are also more vivid, with some showing how deeply animals might be entangled in the emotional lives of their owners. Hence the *Odyssey* (*c*.800 BCE) gives us the moving figure of Argus (Watchful), the dog who patiently waits for Odysseus' return to Ithaca; on finally seeing his master after two decades, he wags his tail once before dying.[14] Similarly striking is Aethon (Fiery), Pallas' war-horse in Virgil's *Aeneid* (19 BCE), who follows the funeral procession of his fallen master with 'tears splashing his face in enormous drops' ('lacrimans guttisque umectat grandibus ora').[15] In fact, the literary and archaeological record is sufficiently extensive to preserve the names of some unusual or exotic beasts, such as Euploia (Good-ship), a seal depicted in a third-century mosaic at Kos, or Porphyrios (Giant, or Purple-one), the whale who menaced the harbours of Byzantium during the reign of Justinian (527–65).[16]

Naturally enough, the greater quantity of Greek and Latin zoonyms allows a larger range of properties to be identified within them. Perhaps the first feature they make clear is how heavily conventionalised animal names tend to be even at this early stage in their history. Some authors

call attention to this point directly. Plutarch reports that the name Hermes (i.e., Anubis) was invariably given to dogs in first-century Egypt.[17] The author of the *Etymologicum Genuinum* (*c.*850 CE), citing a lost work by Aristophanes, likewise claims that Bucephalus was the standard name in Thessaly for every horse branded with an ox-head.[18] Other sources point to these rules by deliberately subverting them. Two key examples are the Homeric burlesque the *Batrachomyomachia* (*c.*400 BCE) and the legal parody *Testamentum Porcelli* (*c.*300 CE). The first recounts a day-long battle between Physignathus (Cheek-puffer), king of the frogs, and the mouse-king Psicharpax (Larder-raider), and mentions the warriors Borborocetes (Marsh-lurker), Pelusius (Slimy), Lichopinax (Bowl-licker), Tyroglyphus (Cheese-nibbler), and so on; the second pretends to be the will of Grunnius Corocatta (Grunter Dog-wolf), a piglet about to be slaughtered, and lists his signatories and beneficiaries as Lardio (Fatty), Ofellicus (Rump), Tergillus (Crackling) and Quirina (Squealer).[19] In either case, the main driver of the humour is obviously the jarring application of elaborate titles to creatures that usually fall outside human nomenclature; the texts therefore take the existence of a set of norms for granted, making it the starting-point for their mockery.[20]

More usually, however, these conventions can be inferred from the repetition of names across multiple sources. The earliest hint of standardisation occurs as far back as Homer's *Iliad* (*c.*800 BCE), where numerous horse-names recur in the chariot teams of Hector, Menelaus and Achilles. Of the eight names Homer gives to war-horses, two – Xanthos (Blonde, or River) and Podargos (Quick-footed) – appear twice, the former in the teams of Hector and Achilles, the latter in the teams of Achilles and Menelaus.[21] While Homer's characters exchange horses at times, these repeated names are unlikely to refer to the same creatures, given that their owners represent different factions in the Trojan war; more likely they draw from, and point to, a fixed lexicon of equestrian names. Similar repetition is found in one of the most significant repositories of dog-names in antiquity, Ovid's description of Actaeon's hunting-pack in the *Metamorphoses* (*c*.8 CE).[22] Many of Ovid's hound-names occur elsewhere: we find his Melampus (Black-paw) and Laelaps (Whirlwind) in Hyginus' *Fabula* (*c*.50 BCE), Harpyia (Ravenous) in Julius Pollux's *Onomasticon* (*c*.190 CE), Hylactor (Barker) in Virgil's *Eclogues* (*c*.38 BCE), and Lacon (Spartan) in Columella's list of approved hound-names from *De re rustica* (*c*.60 CE).[23] His Lycisce (Wolf) is even more generously attested: the name is also given to dogs by Virgil, Aeschylus and Simonides of Ceos, the latter two writing in the fifth century BCE.[24] Outside the *Metamorphoses*, other canine names share similar currency. Ormí (Dash) appears in hunting treatises by Xenophon (*c*.350 BCE) and Arrian (*c*.140 CE) as a suitable name for a swift or perceptive dog; the variant Órmenos also occurs in a hunting scene on the François Vase (*c*.565 BCE).[25] Horse-names act in the same way: the name of Pallas' horse in the *Aeneid* echoes that of Hector's charger Aethe in the *Iliad*.[26] While some of these overlaps are doubtless deliberate allusions, they imply an approved vocabulary of zoonyms, dictated by custom. At the very least they suggest that only certa n names or types of name were deemed suitable for animals.

These tacit restrictions become even clearer when we look at the meanings of the names themselves. Most of the surviving names from antiquity can be grouped into

a small number of categories. The majority are functional in nature and tend, like the Egyptian names before them, to reflect actual or ideal traits. For example, among Xenophon's recommendations are names such as Phónax (Shouter) and Kráugi (Cryer) that emphasise the sound of a dog, Nóis (Sense) or Gnómi (Wisdom) that describe its perspicacity, Polýs (Mighty) or Rómi (Strength) that point to its physical power, or Spoudí (Hasten) or Brýas (Spurt) that pertain to its speed. Ovid likewise labels dogs Canache (Noisemaker), Dorceus (Observant), Dromas (Racer), Thoos (Fast) and Nebrophonos (Deer-killer), while Columella suggests Celer (Quick) and Alkí (Force). A second-century altar now in the churchyard of St Rocco at Gallicano follows similar conventions, bidding the viewer: 'behold the tomb of genial Aeolis [Nimble], for whom I grieve beyond measure' ('Aeolidis tumulum festivae cerne catellae, quam dolui inmodice').[27] It is not only dogs who receive this type of appellation: the emperors Caligula and Lucius Verus are supposed to have kept horses called Incitatus (Galloping) and Volucer (Flyer).[28] As well as stating these virtues explicitly, names might express them in metaphoric or allusive terms. Hence an idyll written in imitation of Theocritus around the second century BCE concerns a shepherd chiding his dog Lámpoure (Lantern) for failing to show the vigilance that his name implies.[29] An important subset of Xenophon's names likewise uses military vocabulary to denote aggression, perceptiveness or speed: Xífon (Swordsman), Lóchos (Ambush), Phýlax (Guardsman), Lonchí (Javelin) and Aichmí (Arrowhead). Natural phenomena or wild creatures serve the same purpose elsewhere: cases in point are Homer's Aethe (Heavenly fire),

Ovid's Aello (Storm), Columella's Lupa (She-wolf), Hyginus' Draco (Dragon) and Mnasalcas of Plataeae's mare Aithyias (Shearwater).[30] Figures from mythology or history are also used to evoke the same qualities. Hyginus lists the dog-names Gorgo (Gorgon) and Zephyrus (West-wind), and mosaics depict fighting boars labelled Gorgonis, Polyneices and Solon, presumably because they equalled their legendary namesakes in ferocity or cunning.[31] In the same vein are Antiochus' elephants Ajax and Patroclus, perhaps named for their strength or loyalty.[32]

Alongside these behavioural names, a second important grouping looks to the physical traits of their referents, especially but not exclusively their coloration. Among Homer's horses are Balios (Piebald) and Lampos (Grey); likewise, Oinás (Wine-stained) features among Xenophon's dog-names, Kirrá (Blond) appears among Arrian's, and Leucon (White), Asbolos (Sooty), Melanchaetes (Dark-coated) and Sticte (Spotted) are among Ovid's hounds. The same tendency can be seen in the unique series of ox-names preserved on a set of clay tablets found at Knossos, and generally dated to *c*.1400 BCE: among the nine or ten names recorded here are Ke-re-no (Dark), Wo-nc-qo-so-qe (Wine-face) and Re-pa-ko-qe (Light-coat).[33] Much like the more utilitarian names, names based on physical appearance frequently take metaphoric form. As well as Xenophon's Phlégon (Blazing) and Augó (Daybreak), appellatives of this type often feature on monuments to Roman pets. In the British Museum is an elaborate second-century marble epitaph for Margarita (Pearl), a Gaulish lapdog expressly praised for her 'snowy body' ('niveo corpore'); the Musée des Jacobins holds another tablet from third-century Aquitaine that is

dedicated to Myia (Gnat), a dog small enough to lay in her mistress' lap ('in sinu iacebat').[34]

For the most part, these patterns reconfirm a point made clear by the Egyptian and medieval examples. Like the earlier and later zoonyms, they show how tightly animal identity and animal usage are fused. A name such as Incitatus or Gnómi very directly conflates the creature with the role its human owners require of it – the watchdog becomes its vigilance, the hunting hound its aggression, the horse its speed, the elephant its brawn, and so on. All are reduced to their function by a form of synecdoche; the behaviours attractive to human beings become defining characteristics. Much the same impulse can be inferred from the descriptive names. After all, what unites these labels is a concern with the bodies of their referents: they also define creatures in terms of their physiology, making their physical properties the basis of identity. It is not difficult to see this approach also resting on a sense that the animal is a material resource above all, a set of muscles or teeth if it is a working animal, or a source of pleasurable tactility if it is a pet.[35] In other words, virtually all these names reiterate the essential point that utility is never far from view when human language interpellates beasts.

Nevertheless, the presence of these conventions does not prevent classical naming from acting in some surprising ways, especially when its relationship to species is considered. While we might expect naming to reflect species-categories, this is not always the case. To be sure, some sources suggest that names ought to be tailored to particular types of creature. We have already seen Plutarch's remarks on Egyptian dog-naming; Xenophon similarly advises that canine names should be carefully customised and selected for brevity and ease of recollection. The same advice is echoed by Columella three centuries later, who adds that dog-names should ideally 'be pronounced with two syllables' ('quae duabus syllabis enuntientur'). There are also hints that agricultural beasts were named differently to hunting hounds and war-horses. The former often have markedly more prosaic appellations: a pastoral by Theocritus from *c.*250 BCE mentions the calf Kymaítha (Chubby), while the Knossos tablets include the oxen To-ma-ko (Mouthy) and A3-zo-ro-qe (Ugly).[36] However, it is equally clear that some names were applied indifferently to multiple species. The heroic name Leander, for example, is given to a bear in a mosaic at Curubis, and to a dog in another mosaic from the villa-complex of Maternus at Carranque.[37] Podargos is a member of the chariot-teams of Menelaus and Achilles in the *Iliad*, another horse in an epitaph recorded in *c.*100 CE, and an ox on the Knossos tablets.[38] The closely-related designations Wo-no-qo-so-qe (Wine-face) and Oinás (Wine-stained) are also applied to oxen and dogs, while Balios is given to dogs and horses, and Lépargos (Light-coat) to oxen and cows.[39] This hopping between species suggests that many zoonyms recognise little distinction between types of animal, or do not regard them as sufficiently important to restrict their significance: that is, while certain names are accepted as germane for particular animals, others seem to denote beasts in general. It might be said that they recall Derrida's idea that the very concept of animal represents a wilful 'confusion of all non-human living creatures' into a single category.[40] As we shall see, this feature becomes even more pronounced in the Middle Ages, where names gain a still greater degree of elasticity.

The fluidity of ancient zoonyms also registers in other ways. As we saw in our last chapter, appellatives do not only reflect the real-world uses to which animals were put, but also have uses of their own: an animal name will often generate complex effects within the text that cites it. While we have already seen something of this tendency in the medieval records, the names from antiquity show the profusion of meanings zoonyms might carry. This point is especially evident in historiography. Classical historians tend to name animals in one of two circumstances: either in connection with celebrated rulers, or with those infamous for their tyranny. In the former class are the animals of Alexander the Great: Bucephalas (Ox-head), the wild horse tamed by the king in his youth, Peritas (January?), the hound in whose honour he founded a city, and Ajax, the elephant captured at the Battle of the Hydaspes.[41] A similar case is Borysthenus (River-nymph), the horse to whom Hadrian dedicated a column.[42] At the other extreme are animals linked with emperors notorious for cruelty or incompetence. The earliest example, and likely model for later writers, is Incitatus, the stallion whom Caligula considered making consul according to Suetonius.[43] In the same vein, Dio Cassius records that Caracalla shared his table and bed with a lion named Akinakes (Short-sword), while Ammianus Marcellinus claims that Valentinian I kept two caged bears called Mica Auream (Nugget) and Innocentia (Innocence) outside his bed-chamber.[44] The *Historia Augusta* (*c*.400 CE) also reports that Lucius Verus doted on a horse named Volucer, while Procopius gives Honorius a pet cockerel called Rómi (Strength).[45] Slightly later, classical Arabic makes reference to Abū Qays, pet monkey of the Umayyad caliph Yazid ibn

Mu'awiya, who would ride a she-ass in his master's drunken horse-races.[46]

Regardless of whether these animals existed, it is not difficult to determine why authors choose to mention them. Peritas, Bucephalus, and Ajax are perhaps the most obvious cases: not only do they directly reflect Alexander's conquests and personal attributes, and so cement his accomplishments as a commander, but they also magnify his status in more general ways, implying that even the most trivial aspects of his biography warrant attention. Borysthenus is likewise a prop for Hadrian's reputation. The other creatures are similarly rhetorical, even if they achieve directly opposing effects. The examples relating to the brutish Caracalla, the ineffectual Valentinian, and the insane Caligula speak for themselves, but all the names in this second group serve critical ends. Rómi, for instance, is used by Procopius to paint Honorius as dangerously deluded: hearing that Rome had been sacked by Alaric, the emperor reputedly fretted over the safety of his pet rather than the fall of the city, 'so great, they say, was the folly with which this emperor was possessed'.[47] Abū Qays is likewise an index of his master's depravity, and part of a larger portfolio of scandalous behaviours: al-Ya'qūbī records that Yazid's 'wantonness' and 'play with monkeys' cost him several allies, while Abū Hamzā al-Sharī blasts him as 'Yazid of the monkeys, a man licentious of stomach, blameworthy of genitals'.[48] Even Lucius Verus, despite his posthumous deification, is ridiculed by the *Historia* through his affection for Volucer: the text depicts him feeding the horse on grapes and nuts, and interprets his obsessive dedication to the creature as decadence equal to Nero's.[49] In all these cases,

there is a clear weaponisation of animal-naming, and of the blurring of human and non-human it implies. Named animals mirror a general erosion of proper order, or show unworthy leaders sliding to the level of unreasoning beasts. But the central point here is the range of meanings classical writers locate in zoonyms. Not only does their work underscore the symbolic potency of animals once they cross into language, but it highlights the plurality of meanings they might express. They show that animals are as versatile a linguistic resource as they are a material one.

Even this brief survey should make clear that there are various points at which classical animal names foreshadow medieval convention. Both periods show how powerfully use-value affects language when it engages with non-human organisms, and show its influence playing out in parallel ways: names in both periods are conventionalised, comic, affective and above all expressive of the demands humans make on beasts. Much of this can be attributed to larger continuities in practice across the periods, which remained fairly stable until the mechanisation of agriculture, transport and warfare in the nineteenth and twentieth centuries. It is only to be expected that designations remained relatively stable when animals themselves performed much the same roles in the classical, medieval and, indeed, early modern worlds. But equally significant is Greece and Rome's formative impact on the medieval records. It barely needs stating how reliant medieval writing was on classical models and material: not only were ancient *auctores* every pupil's entry-point into literacy throughout the Middle Ages, but the entire framework of education, with its sequential movement between discrete *artes liberales*, was rooted in late antiquity.[50] Put simply, the ancient world is bound to condition the way in which names were recorded and evaluated in the Middle Ages, merely as part of its all-pervading influence on writing itself.

Some of this can be seen in the most direct legacy of the classical world – its mythography, and the learned debates that evolved out of and around it. Named animals occur in numerous Greek and Roman myths. Some of the earliest are found in the cycle of stories around Heracles: the demigod's animal opponents include Orthus, herding-dog of Eurytion, and Phaéthon (Bright), a bull of Augeas who attempted to gore the hero during the fifth of his labours.[51] Plutarch also mentions the wild sow Phaea in his life of Theseus, although speculates that she may have been a female bandit distorted by oral tradition.[52] Similarly, Callimachus gives the name Almathea (Sweet-goddess) to the nanny goat who fed the infant Zeus, although Musaeus, Eratosthenes and other authorities make her the goat's owner.[53] Pseudo-Apollodorus likewise calls Erigone's dog Maira (Flash) when recounting the murder of her father Icarius by drunken shepherds.[54]

In the context of the later period, however, these narratives are less interesting for their content than for the way in which they present their material. As they move between sources, these stories exhibit a great deal of fluidity: mythographers often treat them as loose frameworks, switching out their names at will. Kleitias' depiction of the hunt for the Calydonian Boar on the François Vase is one early example: Kleitias adds labels to seven of Meleager's hounds, giving them such names as Lábros (Fury), Kóraks (Raven) and Égértes (Watchful).[55] A similar tack is assumed

by the mosaics at Carranque: when depicting the death of Adonis at the tusks of a boar, they dub Adonis' dogs Leander and Titurus, perhaps after Maternus' own hounds.[56] But probably the supreme example of this porosity is the story of Actaeon, the huntsman torn apart by his own hounds.[57] Assigning names to Actaeon's pack becomes a sort of intellectual game in antiquity. Aside from Ovid's list of thirty-six hounds, the second-century *Bibliotheka* gives a sequence of six names, Julius Pollux quotes four names from Aeschylus' lost tragedy *Toxotides*, and Hyginus assembles two distinct lists, one echoing the *Metamorphoses*, the other piecing together forty-six names from undisclosed 'other authors' ('alii auctores'). In fact, the practice of grafting new names into myths probably accounts for the variations that trouble some ancient commentators. In Pliny's discussion of canine loyalty, for instance, three separate creatures are linked with the story of a royal dog who jumped into his dead master's pyre: Pyrrhus (Fiery), dog of Gelon of Syracuse, Hyrcanus (Hyrcanian), dog of Lysimachus of Thrace, and an anonymous dog of Hiero I of Syracuse.[58] Pliny's confusion again points to the permeability of myth, and its tendency to attract new content as it circulates.

What makes these games of musical chairs all the more significant is that they inspire similar manoeuvres in the later period. When medieval authors engage with classical stories, they also approach them not as static facts, but as outlines that can be populated with their own choice of names. Sometimes this process leans towards outright parody, as in the Ovidian burlesques of *Ysengrimus* and Chaucer's *Nun's Priest's Tale*, but even sober imitations will insert contemporary names into the narratives they adapt:

hence the *Ovide Moralisé* (*c*.1300) includes French names in its version of the Actaeon episode, while traditional English equivalents appear in Golding's and Sandys's translations further down the track. The sequence of German names given to a poacher's hounds in the *Gesta Romanorum* (*c*.1300) or the sixty hounds owned by Earl Iron in *Thidrek's Saga* (*c*.1250) might also follow Ovid's lead.[59] Each of these cases is an important collection of medieval names in its own right, and is no doubt authorised by the malleability of the classical stories. Mythography did not merely give the Middle Ages a precedent for recording appellatives, in other words, but also gave it a blueprint by which it could record its own conventions.

But elsewhere the relationship between classical example and medieval imitation operates along different lines, and highlights some of the social determinants that shape appellation. Especially important here are elegies for dead pets. The classical memorial elegy seems to have emerged around the fifth century BCE: the earliest surviving example is Simonides of Ceos' epitaph for Lykas (Wolf), a Thessalian hunting dog.[60] Its popularity seems to have been cemented by the third century BCE: from this date come Mnasalcas of Plataeae's verse on Aithyias, and two verses attributed to Tymnes of Crete, one paying tribute to the song-bird Elaeus and the other to Tauron (Bull), a watchdog named presumably for his bark.[61] The form remained fashionable throughout antiquity, giving rise to tablets and inscriptions across the Roman empire, usually for dogs: as well as those set up for Myia at Aquitaine and Margarita at Gaul, surviving monuments honour Parthenope (Siren) at Byzantium, Fuscus (Dark) at modern-day Oderzo, Aminnaracus in Wales,

Heuresis (Finder) near the via Tiburtina, and Patrice (From the Fatherland) at Salerno.[62] There are also a number of further examples of unknown provenance, such as marbles for Theia (Goddess) and Helena.[63] The form is so well known by the first century that it becomes subject to parody. While Catullus' homage to Lesbia's sparrow is relatively po-faced, Martial's epigram on Issa (Herself) is more obviously mocking, claiming that her master Publius thought her entirely 'innocent of sexuality' ('ignorat Venerem'); his later verse on the hunting bitch Lydia is however more straightforward.[64] In fact, even animals who did not command particular affection might be memorialised: Dio Chrysostom quotes an inscription to a dog named Líthargos (Lazy).[65]

Although this form also furnishes medieval authors with another fertile model for preserving zoonyms, its influence plays out in a different way. There is little evidence that this practice extended organically into the Middle Ages. Memorials in the early medieval period are too sporadic to suggest a continuous tradition: the few examples that do exist are anomalous geographic outliers, such as the pillar erected for Puníśa, a hunting-dog killed by boar at Phalāram Gollarahatti, or the Ātakūr inscription for Kāli (Goddess of Death), another hound killed hunting boar by the Tungabhadra river in 804 CE.[66] The memorial only begins to reappear in earnest in western Europe in the late fifteenth century, and perceptibly as a self-conscious revival. One of the earliest examples is the brief verse of *c.*1480 composed in imitation of Martial by Jacques de Brézé, count of Maulevrier, for 'the beautiful white racing-dog' Souillart.[67] From around the same date is an epigram on the lapdog Zabot, tellingly but doubtfully attributed to the pioneering humanist Petrarch: 'dear Zabot, for you is a small home and a shallow grave, since you had but a small body; receive also this brief song'.[68]

However, a key centre for memorialisation was the ducal court of Mantua in the early sixteenth century, where a cult seems to have grown up around the pets of Isabella d'Este and her children; it is unlikely to be a coincidence that the court was also a leading centre of humanism and artistic patronage.[69] In 1510 Mario Equicola staged an elaborate funeral for Isabella's cat Martino, causing Battista Scalona to give a sardonic account of how 'poor Martino of blessed memory' was interred 'with the universal grief of the court'.[70] Even more extravagant were the obsequies marking the death of the dog Aura (Gold) a year later: her death inspired a sequence of seventy-six elegies from Isabella's circle of court-poets.[71] Other dogs received similar honours: among the epitaphs transcribed by Aldrovandi in the seventeenth century are dedications for Zephyro, Fanina, Mamie, Viola, Rubinus and Bellina.[72] One of these memorials has in fact survived as a physical artefact, in the form of a marble designed by Giulio Romano in 1526 to honour 'Oriana, a little dog, divine in form, loyalty and play'.[73] Such self-aware acts of imitation obviously expose another front at which antiquity touched on medieval onomastics. Yet they also show how this contact did not affect the later period in a uniform way. Memorialisation might have provided another model for preserving the names of pets, but its influence was obviously limited to the privileged, intellectual levels of medieval culture; a smallholder of Maulevrier is unlikely to have commissioned an epitaph for his cow or herding-dog. As a result, they spell out how tightly the language

of animals is bound up with the same economic determinants that shape their treatment, and how naming is no less hierarchised than the society in which it is performed.

Nevertheless, while these continuities are illuminating, equally crucial are the points at which the Middle Ages veer away from classical precedent. Despite its heavy debt to antiquity, several conventions were not integrated into medieval custom. One of the most visible of these departures concerns religion. In classical naming, a small but sizeable number of zoonyms look to the pantheon to find metaphors for a creature's physical characteristics. While this inclination is most conspicuous in the Egyptian sources, Greek and Roman authors also look to their own deities: as well as the whale Porphyrios and lapdog Theia, the Carthaginian poet Luxorius alludes to a boar named Mars, Julius Pollux and Hyginus include Charon and Zephyrus among their dog-names, and the fourth-century mosaics at Cos depict a bull named Aeris, a stag named Eros, and a bear named Dionysios.[74] Needless to say, there is no evidence of any comparable habit among medieval names. Outside the surreal world of allegory, where a writer such as Langland can name Piers Plowman's oxen after the four evangelists, mingling the sacred and bestial was anathema to the later period.[75] There are times at which animals are specifically forbidden identities touching on devotional ideology. An emblematic case is St Guinefort, the greyhound supposedly killed in error by his master, who became the centre of a peasant cult in thirteenth-century Lyon.[76] When he uncovered the identity of this mysterious local martyr, the Dominican preacher Stephen of Bourbon was sufficiently horrified to have Guinefort's shrine destroyed and his cult suppressed.[77] Although medieval writers were happy to muddy the distinction between human and animal, they were less willing to confuse the animal and divine.

But more significant still is a cluster of zoonyms that has no exact equivalent in the Middle Ages, simply because the practices associated with it do not extend beyond the Roman world. Of particular note in this respect are the names given to exotic animals in visual depictions of the staged hunts known as *venationes*. Hence the Rudston Venus mosaic, originally part of a third-century villa in East Yorkshire, features a bull labelled Omicida (Murder) and a lion called either Flammefer (Blaze) or Frammefer (Spear-carrier) depending on how the surviving tesserae are interpreted.[78] Further mosaics and frescoes at Cos, Curubis, Radez and Smirat include the bears Drakontis (Snakelike), Tachine (Swiftly), Invictus (Unconquered) and Itus (Charging), and the leopards Victor (Winner), Crispinus (Curly) and Luxurius (Excitable), along with similarly named seals and boars.[79]

There is little evidence that medieval culture conferred names on animals of this kind, for the simple reason that it had no customs exactly corresponding to the Roman games. Its own blood sports, although numerous, tended not to take the same semi-theatrical form: although ritualised in their own way, medieval hunts did not conceive their quarries as actors in quasi-dramatic spectacles. The closest parallel to the *venatio* is bearbaiting, which did occasionally name its reluctant stars. Bosse (Lump?) seems to have been standard for a performing bear by the fourteenth century, when it is used in *Richard the Redeless* (*c.*1399) to satirise the Earl of Warwick; its widespread usage can be inferred

from the nickname of a public fountain at Billingsgate, 'dubbed Bossa by common people' owing to its bearlike shape.[80] After baiting found a permanent venue at the 'Paryse garden' in Southwark in the 1540s, such named bears as Sekerson, Tom Hunckes, Ben Hunt and Nan Talbot became staples of Tudor popular literature.[81] Yet these instances are merely exceptions that prove the general rule. On the whole the Middle Ages did not join antiquity in applying names to leopards, boars and seals because it saw no need to do so, finding no use for these creatures that required their interpellation. Consequently, the Roman fighting animals again point to the decisive role that utility plays in naming. Not only individual creatures but entire species will fall outside nomination if they lie beyond a culture's resourcefulness.

All told, classical sources carry several implications for interpreting the practices of the later period. Although we might think of animal-naming in the Middle Ages as purely colloquial, closer scrutiny suggests otherwise. The ways in which classical languages deal with animals, and the identities that they construct for non-human creatures, have a high level of tenacity. These analogies are not merely coincidental, or the result of a kind of folk-memory; rather, they reflect the extent to which classical thinking suffused medieval literate culture. It is worth remembering that most of our knowledge of the Middle Ages comes from what its authors have chosen to tell us, and that their sense of what was worthy of record is invariably coloured by their training and the exemplars they inherited. The paradoxical result is that the Middle Ages often finds license to discuss its own experiences in the parameters laid down by antiquity. If anything, zoonyms show the depth of this influence, demonstrating that even the most mundane aspects of daily life might conceal older ideas and frameworks, although their impact naturally varies across lines of class and region. Above and beyond these factors, however, the classical sources make a much broader point. They remind us that zoonyms, while they might appear innocent and inconsequential, are in reality trapdoors that open into multiple meanings – meanings that might be cultural, economic, political or theological, as well as practical. Much as Augustus and Aemilius Paullus assumed, zoonyms do indeed reveal obscure truths.

CHAPTER 4

TYPE CASTING:
NAMING AND SPECIES

WHEN WE THINK about species today, and the hierarchies into which living things can be arranged, we tend to do so in the terms set down by eighteenth- and nineteenth-century naturalists. From the work of Linnaeus comes the meticulous division of organisms into distinct groups, each with a binomial Latin tag; from Cuvier comes an emphasis on comparative anatomy, particularly the configuration of organs.[1] From Darwin and his followers comes the idea that speciation is itself a responsive process, a sort of dialogue with environment in which 'better adaptation ... to the surrounding physical conditions' ensures survival.[2] We might also visualise the natural order in the diagrammatic form popularised by Darwin and Haeckel, and familiar from countless school textbooks – as a phylogenetic 'tree', with *homo sapiens* at the top, the great apes on the neighbouring branches, and the remaining creatures a series of wrong-turns fanning outwards from the trunk.[3]

As might be expected, medieval scholars took a different approach.[4] This is not to say that their conclusions differ from later thinking completely. The Middle Ages obviously recognised the physical variety of living things; most intellectuals of the period would agree that beings

could be stacked vertically in a chain or *scala naturae*, even though they tended to group creatures according to the elements that they inhabited instead of line of descent.[5] They would likewise accept the placement of the human being over other organisms, given that Judeo-Christian tradition stresses Adam's 'dominion' over 'the beasts, and the whole earth' (Genesis 1:26). But medieval thought parts company with Darwinism when it looks to the next rung down the ladder, and considers which creatures most resemble human beings. For many writers on zoology, the closest animals to humankind were not the chimpanzee and bonobo, but the dog and the horse. The *locus classicus* of these ideas is Isidore of Seville's great seventh-century encyclopaedia the *Etymologiae*.[6] When referring to the dog, Isidore elevates it above the rest of the animal kingdom by virtue of its intellect, asserting that 'nothing is wiser than dogs; they have greater sense than other animals'. Such is the extent of this 'wisdom', he argues, that it allows the dog to partake in the supremely human privileges of language and social organisation: 'they alone recognise their names; they love their lords; they defend the home of their lord'.[7] The horse for its part demonstrates similar affinities, although in its emotional rather than linguistic faculties:

> The vitality of horses is great: for they exult in the field; they catch the scent of warfare; they are roused to battle by the sound of the trumpet; they are compelled to race by a loud voice; they are saddened when they are defeated; they rejoice when they have won ... when their masters are killed or dying, many shed tears. For only a horse can weep for a man and feel the emotion of grief.[8]

In fact, such is the horse's closeness to human levels of sensitivity and duty that it is possible for the two species to merge: Isidore concludes by referring to the mythic centaurs, which he notes 'intermingled the natures of horses and men'.[9] In either case, the proximity to human beings is not determined by biological similarity, but in terms of the perceived capacities of animals to think and feel like human beings.

This thinking might provoke several reactions from us today. It may simply appear ludicrous: to some extent the *Etymologiae* recalls Borges's parodic taxonomy that so amused Foucault, where the natural world is similarly divided into such arbitrary ranks as 'those that tremble as if they were mad' or 'those that from a distance resemble flies'.[10] We might dismiss it as unscientific: direct observation clearly takes a backseat to literary tradition in Isidore's system, since most of his 'facts' about weeping horses and sagacious dogs are merely culled from Virgil and Pliny. It might even strike us as ethically objectionable: the fact that Isidore privileges creatures on the basis of their being 'most like us' looks forward to the central problem Carey Wolfe identifies in later animal rights philosophy.[11] Nonetheless, in some respects, it can be said that Isidore's reasoning rests on a more honest idea of human-animal relationships than many subsequent frameworks. After all, unless one happens to be a zookeeper, poacher or warden in a wildlife refuge, few people today are likely to have regular contact with orangutans or gorillas, despite sharing genetic ancestry with them. Indeed, the primates' proximity to *homo sapiens* has not led to any exemption from the exploitation, cruelty and indifference that governs most animal-human interactions, something their shrinking habitats and usage in medical testing can attest. In a sense, Isidore offers a truer sense of where the human and animal meet, looking beyond anatomical resemblance towards more concrete and practical pinch-points.

But more importantly, Isidore's thinking spills over into the naming systems of the Middle Ages. Its most visible impact is on the distribution of the records themselves. In numeric terms, the surviving names directly mirror his zoological hierarchy, also awarding pre-eminence to dogs and horses. It is in fact hard to overstate the extent to which names for these creatures dominate over all others, running to hundreds, even thousands of items, and pushing all other zoonyms into a small minority. Much as Isidore remarks, horses and dogs were neighbouring species as far as medieval people were concerned, being firmly enmeshed in their lives and language. However, these looser, pre-Enlightenment classifications also impress themselves on naming in more subtle ways as well. This chapter will unpick the relationship between the two, working through the names medieval culture assigned to particular orders of creature, and drawing out the logic that governs them. As we shall see, appellatives shed considerable light on the ways in which animals were grouped and differentiated in the period, and lay bare the dense matrix of factors that underpinned its organisation of the animal world.

HOUND'S TONGUES: DOG-NAMES

To start at the top of Isidore's hierarchy, medieval canine names are not only remarkable for their extent, but their extraordinary range. This diversity can be glimpsed in the records of the 1504 Zurich lottery. The dog-names listed here straddle an impressive range of categories: they evoke the mythic figures Artus (Arthur) and Melesinn (Melusine), beasts such as Betzli (Little-bear) or Fötschli (Little-fish), characteristics such as Fröid (Joy) or Trüb (Sober), physical features such as Rot Kron (Red Crown) and Menly (Little-one), and even include joke-names such as Nieman (Nobody) and Wass du (Hey you).[12] To some extent, this variety is an effect of the records themselves. With few exceptions, dog-names tend to appear in lists, many inspired by Ovid or Columella. Examples include Michelangelo Biondo's chapter on 'new-minted names for dogs' ('neotericis nominibus canis') in *De Canibus et venatione* (1544), and the catalogues appended to manuscripts of De Brézé's *Les Dits du bon Chien Souillard* (*c*.1480) and Edward of York's *Master of Game* (*c*.1414).[13] But the variability of dog-names also mirrors the wide range of demands that medieval culture made on dogs. As Corinne Beck and Fabrice Guizard point out, the medieval dog is not a singular entity, but one refracted by expertise ('compétence') and social position ('statut social').[14] Something of this can be seen in John Gower's *Visio Anglie* (1381), with its nightmare vision of an animal uprising. When Gower surveys the legions of dogs turning against their masters, he ranks them not by breed but according to activity and social class:[15]

> They do not run across the woods to snatch up a hare, nor do they pursue stags ... Cutte and Curre raced together madly through backstreets, leaving their poor homes destitute. Look! There appears the shepherd's dog, and he that barks at night and keeps courtyards safe: these

two roundly commit mischief. In every bakery and in every kitchen the chain is broken and turns loose its dog. I saw the butcher's great bandog drawing near; nor does the mill dog remain at home. Neither can the stable restrain retired barkers, as they too join their allies.[16]

Gower is not alone in differentiating dogs along these lines, although other authors are more systematic. In the sixteenth century, Biondo also sorts dogs according to purpose and status. His categories consist of four main 'varieties of dog' ('genere canis'): watchdogs ('canis defensorius'), sheepdogs ('canis pastoris'), hunting dogs ('canis venaticus') and small dogs ('catuli') that are 'darlings of the prince, and of matrons' ('delicias et Principum, et Matronarum').[17]

The same factors also determine the types of name that dogs are allocated. While there is some flexibility, names tend to fall into three broad classes. First, dogs kept as pets are usually named in ways that denote their emotional value, or their incorporation into the household or family. Many of their designations are straightforward endearments. Judging from the lettering carved on his collar, Bo (Beau) was the name of a dog belonging to Sir John Reynes and his wife Catherine, on whose c.1428 monument at Clifton Reynes he appears; likewise, David Lyndsay reports that James V's favoured pet, who habitually 'lyis on the Kingis nycht gown', was known as Bawtie (Beauty).[18] Others are shortened versions of anthroponyms: the memorial brasses of Lady Alicia Cassy (d. 1401) at Deerhurst and of Sir Brian de Stapleton (d.1448) at Ingham depict spaniels labelled Terri and Iakke (Jack), while Margaret Paston owned a dog named Hankyn (Jonny) in the 1470s.[19] Some names go further still in humanising their referents, at times tipping over into outright infantilisation. An early instance is Petitcrieu (Little-cry), the enchanted lapdog Tristram gives to Isolde in Gottfried von Strassbourg's *Tristan* (*c*.1200), but a more interesting case is a dog owned by Anne Boleyn.[20] Although popular histories typically call him Purkoy (Pourquoi, i.e., Why?), giving rise to the myth that he was named for his quizzical expression, his name should properly read Purboy (Pure-boy).[21] Writing to Viscountess Lisle on the creature's death in December 1534, and quoting the courtier Margery Lyster as his source, the MP Thomas Broke clearly uses this spelling: 'the Queynys grace settyth muche store by a prety dogge, and her grace delytyd so muche in lytle Purboy that after he was ded of a fall there durst no body tell her grace of it, tyll it pleassyd the kynges highness to tell her grace.'[22] The same childlike style of naming occurs further afield. In her *Makura no Sōshi* (*c*.1000 CE) Sei Shōnagon relates the story of Okinamaro, a palace dog exiled by the Heian emperor Ichijō for chasing a favourite cat, whose name translates to 'Silly Old Boy'.[23] Nonetheless, the quasi-filial ties that define pet/owner relationships are not the sole determinants of naming. Some names symbolise affluence instead, probably because lapdogs themselves were the preserve of social elites. Dogs at the Mantuan court included Rubinus (Ruby) and Aura (Gold), while Henry IV of France reputedly kept a puppy named after a different order of luxury item: Citron (Lemon) apparently shared the young king's bed.[24]

The names of herders and watchdogs, on the other hand, tend be less intimate and more utilitarian. Perhaps

C

the starkest illustration of this tendency is provided by medieval German, where such animals were simply known as Wacker (Watcher).[25] In 1510 the attack dog who played a role putting down the Taíno rebellion against the Spanish was called Berezillo (Excellent).[26] In English, Gower's brief designations seem to be typical: just as Cutte is a short-ened form of Cuthbert, and Curre a synonym for mastiff, so other working dogs tend to have basic descriptors or hypocoristic versions of human names. A piece of doggerel celebrating the English victory at Calais in 1347 refers to 'the watir-bailiffes dog' Goby (Joby), and an illustration of a herdsman's dog from a fourteenth-century calendar labels the creature Talbat (Hound).[27] Likewise, Colle (Nicky) is used by John Paston II in 1476 as a proverbial name for a guard-dog: commenting on the inadequate defences at Caister castle, Paston grumbles 'ther is no mor in it but Colle and hys mak, and a goose may get it'.[28] Given that another Colle leads the charge against the fox in Chaucer's *Nun's Priest's Tale*, it is probable that this was an accepted name for a watchdog. Early modern sources associate dogs of this rank with similar appellatives: the 'Mastiffes, and Mungrells' that chase a werewolf in Drayton's *Moon-Calfe* (1631) also carry human nicknames or are named after simple traits and habits, such as Hog (from Roger), Ball (from Baldwin or Archibald), Eateall (Eat-all), Cuttaile (Cut-tail) or Blackfoot.[29] Although there is some humanisa-tion at work here, the emotional inflections of these names are markedly lower than those given to pets. Animals with these names are evidently not woven into the family struc-tures or economic identities of their owners to the same extent as domestic canines.

The third major group, dogs used in hunting, is more difficult to generalise, for the simple reason that these names survive in much greater quantities. Medieval culture took obvious delight in generating appellatives for dogs of this kind: the De Brézé catalogue totals sixty-four names, while the list of 'names of all maner of houndis' appended to the *Master of Game* runs to well over a thousand. Their very number is telling. In strictly practical terms, it stands to reason that hounds would require a large volume of care- fully finessed names, given their organisation into packs in which individual dogs still needed to be directed. Such a situation is vividly depicted by the royal huntsman William Twiti in his L'*Art de vénerie* (1327), which advises 'if a hound is on the scent, and the name of that hound is Richer [Strong] or Bemound [Fair-hill], you say "Hark, to Bemonde, yield, hark, hey, to him, yield to him, onward, to Bemond, onward, ho, sir"'.[30] At the same time, however, it also demonstrates the high value of these creatures: the level of creativity run- ning through the lists is testament to the hound's status as an object of play and pleasure.

Accordingly, hound-names are characterised by the elaborate, at times poetic, forms that they take. It is true that some names are relatively straightforward. The hunting pack of Earl Iron in *Thidrek's Saga* (*c.*1250) consists of such bluntly functional names as Luska (Sneaking), Rusca (Barker), Bracka (Tracker) and Porsa (Stalker), while Gunnar's Irish hound in *Njáls saga* (*c.*1300) is simply called Sámur (Dark).[31] Some of the names seen elsewhere were also permissible for hounds and greyhounds: Litilboye, Beawte, Terry, Cutte, Goby and Balle occur on the *Master of Game* list, and Black- foote, Eateal and Cole are used by Golding, Sandys and

Fraunce in their versions of the Actaeon story.[32] Yet many are notable for their level of inventiveness. Several take a metaphoric approach to interpellation, denoting a dog's speed, tracking ability or killing power in emblematic terms not unlike the classical hound-names. A particularly fertile strand of imagery comes from the wider animal kingdom. Noteworthy names of this type include Arthur's dog Caball (Horse) from Nennius' *Historia* (*c*.900 CE), Fionn mac Cumhail's hound Bran (Raven) from *Fhiannaíocht* (*c*.1100), Oyse (Bird) from the De Brézé list, Leo (Lion) and Lupus (Wolf) from Biondo, and Foxe, Cormerawnte, Dolfyn and Mouse from the *Master of Game*.[33] The conquistador Vasco Núñez de Balboa is also said to have used an attack-dog named Leoniça (Lionlike) during his Panamanian expeditions of 1509–13.[34] Natural phenomena are equally favoured: Biondo mentions dogs named Stella (Star) and Fulgur (Lightning), while English sources have Tempest, Whirlwinde, Sykamore and Bleise (Blaze).[35]

But more remarkable is the preponderance of intricate compound forms. This trend can be seen in the two most pervasive names in English, Ryngewode (Wood-echoer) and Kilbucke. Both appear in the *Master of Game* list, and are widely attested over the next few centuries: one or other is used by Fraunce, Chapman, Shakespeare, Richard Robinson, John Harington, Tobias Hume and Izaak Walton, among many others.[36] A variant of Kilbucke also reappears in the story of Gelert, legendary hound of the thirteenth-century prince Llywelyn ab Iorwerth, whose grave supposedly gives the village of Beddgelert its name. The name is evidently a Welsh approximation of the English Kilhart; the earliest reference to his legend uses this spelling when describing the dog's burial 'within the limits of Eivionydd', and adds the explanation that he 'brought down deer in pairs'.[37] Other names conform to the same morphology: it can be seen in Sir Tristran's Husdent (Fine-teeth), Lyndsay's Lanceman, the German names Emulemin (Bear-runner) and Hanegyf (Take-and-give) from the *Gesta Romanorum* (*c*.1300), and the English names Merymowthe (Merry-mouth), Harde-ynowgh (Hardy-enough), Schake-schaw (Forest-shaker) and Havegoodday.[38]

While these examples could be multiplied tenfold, they make abundantly clear how much creative energy medieval culture expended on constructing identities for hounds. These sophisticated coinages, with their carefully drawn images, are an obvious indicator of the value invested in the beasts. However, they also make obvious that hounds are accorded a different value to lapdogs. Hunting dogs are less likely to be personalised: humanlike designations only represent a small proportion of their names, with the majority prizing them for their non-human qualities, and likening them to wild animals and natural forces. But these distinctions also raise a wider point too, underscoring that the dog is more of a set of roles than observable species-characteristics. They lay bare the influence of material usage in classifying these animals; even their variability reflects the broad spread of uses to which dogs were put.

This variation can be further seen in the rhetorical effects dog-names produce.[39] On the one hand, most European languages had at least one canine name that could serve as shorthand for dogs in general, much like Fido or Rover later on: Bodri in Hungarian, Talbot in English, Waldgesell (Forest-companion) in German, and Soldan

C

(Sultan) in Danish all possessed this totemic function.[40] However, named dogs prove unusually rich in the meanings they might express. Like Estula, they can be straightforwardly comic. Domestic dog-names also provide the punchline for one of John Rastell's *Hundred Mery Tales* (*c*.1529): this concerns a schoolboy struggling to resolve the proposition 'Noye had thre sonnes, Sem, Came, and Japhete ... who was Japhetes father?'; his own father helps by explaining that his dog Colle also has three puppies, Ryg, Trygge and Tryboll, and emphasises that Colle therefore 'nedes be syre to Tryboll'; when the boy returns to school, he informs his master that Japheth's father must be 'Colle my fathers dogge'.[41] But as well as taking humorous meanings, named dogs might also be used in political protest. An infamous example is the couplet William Collingbourne made in 1484 to slander Richard III and his councillors William Catesby, Richard Ratcliffe and Francis Lovell: 'The catte, the ratte, and Louell our dogge, rulyth all Englande vnder a hogge'.[42] As Collingbourne is supposed to have argued at trial, albeit without success, Lovell (Love-well) was merely a name 'Dogs haue borne ... of yore', and the name does indeed occur in the *Master of Game* list and *Historie of Iacob and Esau* (1557).[43] Even more macabre is the use to which the dogs Colle, Grubbe, Lugtrype, Slugge and Turne-bole were put in 1456: their severed heads were found mounted in Fleet Street, apparently as an oblique attack on the Duke of York.[44] Like Collingbourne's verse, they show that traditional names could be used aggressively as well as playfully.

However, named dogs can also carry further meanings. In the allegorical poem 'Mirror of the Periods of Man's Life' (*c*.1430), for example, the hunting hound Bemond embodies the louche and pleasure-seeking lifestyle into which youngsters might drift.[45] Rather different meanings are presented by Asterion (Starry), the 'beautiful white dog' ('bel cane bianco') in Iacopo Sannazaro's *Arcadia* (1482), who is loaned by one shepherd to another so that he might participate in country-games: Asterion encapsulates the intellectual and emotional fraternity Sannazaro imagines, with his Greek-derived name and status as symbolic gift.[46] All told, these literary dogs reflect once again the influence of concrete usage. Their appearance in multiple genres parallels the number of practical roles asked of real medieval dogs; comedy, complaint and allegory are merely the literary equivalents of the stable, courtyard and butcher's shop from which Gower's canines erupt.

NEIGH-SAYERS: HORSE-NAMES

Although horse-names cannot compete with dog-names for variety, they are more than a match for ubiquity, appearing in an unparalleled range of contexts. To be sure, some named horses are found in predictable places. It is only to be expected, for instance, that the chivalric romance should feature Gawain's Gryngolet (White-sturdy), El Cid's Bavieca (Barbarian) and William Marshall's Blancart (Pale), given the horse's role in constructing knightly identity; it is not for nothing that 'well horsed and well i-armed' is Thomas Malory's favourite phrase for describing Arthur's warriors.[47] But alongside these sources, named horses crop up in a host of further texts and documents: indeed, their high monetary value makes them the only creatures as likely to appear in wills, inventories and other financial sources as poetry, proverbs and jokes.

This pervasiveness alone is testament to the horse's deep absorption into everyday medieval life. However, for all their diversity, the records tend to fall into two camps. First, equine names in heroic literature tend to resemble hound-names, celebrating virtues and taking complex composite forms. In the *Chanson de Roland* (*c*.1100), the chargers of Charlemagne's paladins and their 'Sarrazin' opponents have densely figurative titles: Charlemagne himself rides Tencendor (Turmoil), while Veillantif (Valiant) and Pessecerf (Deerhunter) carry Roland and Gerers into battle; their enemies likewise ride Barbamusche (Berber-fly), Gramimund (Steep-mount), and Salt Perdut (Sudden leap).[48] Just as colourful are Broieguerre (War-grinder) and Broiefort (Strong-grinder), horses in *Quatre Fils Aymon* (*c*.1190) and *Ogier de Danemarche* (*c*.1215).[49] Outside the epic and romance, other high literary forms interpellate horses in much the same way. When the *Grímnismál* (*c*.950) details the horses that carry the Norse gods to daily judgement, its names include Skeiðbrimir (Fleet-runner), Silfrintoppr (Silver-top), Falhófnir (Hollow-hoof), Gulltoppr (Gold-top) and Alsviðr (All-speed).[50] Other mythopoetic sources add Skinfaxi (Shining-mane), Hrímfaxi (Frost-mane) and Svaðilfara (Dark-traveller).[51] These names are not only marked by their ornate construction, and their emphasis on speed and strength, but by their wilful oddity, as they paint their bearers as singular in their powers.

Conversely, other sources apply less fanciful, more matter-of-fact labels. Texts of a more popular slant allocate horses rough colour-based classifications or shortened human names. Hence Lyarde (Dapple) is the name of a clapped-out carthorse in a ribald poem collected by

Robert Thornton in *c*.1430, while Gyll is a 'mare of good mold' in an equally suggestive ballad of *c*.1540; likewise, Bayard (Bay) is Chaucer's name for a carthorse in *Troilus and Criseyde* (*c*.1386) and the *Reeve's Tale* (*c*.1390), and Scot is the 'ful good stot' ridden by his Reeve.[52] Horse-names in wills, accounts and other documentary sources tend to be equally unglamorous. Examples include Ward (Guardian), left by the woolmonger John Assheford in 1348; Bayard, bequeathed by Robert Bykenore of Dartford in 1365; Merchxa (Dark), sold in 1430 by an agent of Sandalj Hranić, Grand Duke of Bosnia; Yongesorell (Young-sorrel), a courser in a 1398 inventory from Clone Castle; and Aumbler (Ambler) from the 1452 will of Willelmus Nicolas of Charing.[53] Alongside these descriptors and diminutives, there are also a few simple metaphoric names. While these often follow hound-names in looking to the wider animal sphere, their frame of reference is noticeably less exotic. A horse called Porcus (Pig) was surrendered against a debt of two marks in Kraków in 1388, and Brok (Badger) is one of the stubborn drayhorses who provoke their master into damning them to hell in Chaucer's *Friar's Tale*.[54] There is also a much higher degree of repetition among these names. Many recur across multiple sources: another Brok and yet another Bayard appear in the 1458 will of John Wrygh, two further Scots are found in the *Friar's Tale* and the 1451 will of John Bagshall of Featherstone, and a horse named Sorell was left with 'broken bridle' ('freno debiliori') by Johannes de Harwood, lawyer of York, to one of his clerks in 1406.[55] Such repetitiveness is in direct contrast to the other appellations, with their deliberate and emphatic peculiarity.

What we can see, in other words, is a sort of fault-line running through equine naming, separating texts written in a heroic vein from those that are more practical in orientation. The distinction between the two is by no means absolute: despite Bayard's prevalence as a workaday name, its ultimate prototype is Baiart, a stallion of prodigious strength from *Quatre Fils Aymon*.[56] Nonetheless, the sources can be organised into two broad camps, one marked by its elevated language, the other by its pointed lack of flamboyance. The question that naturally arises is whether this division is merely a discursive one, or whether it represents the realities of medieval horse ownership. While this question is difficult to resolve with full confidence, it is still possible to detect authentic practice beneath the divide. Although they differed little in their physical dimensions, the fact is that medieval horses had their own sociology no less than medieval dogs.[57] This point is apparent in Chaucer's *Canterbury Tales*. When Chaucer pictures his pilgrims 'nyne and twenty', and in the process assembles a panoramic cross-section of fourteenth-century society, the horse emerges as a major codifier of rank: more than half of the travellers are defined by the horse they ride, from the Nun's Priest's 'jade ... foul and lene' and the Monk's 'palfrey ... broun as is a berye', to the Knight's 'hors ... goode' and the Clerk's mount 'leene ... as is a rake'.[58] The horse is then a potent status symbol for Chaucer and his readers, providing a clear shorthand for its owner's economic standing. As Heather Dail notes, it is one of the 'silent translators' by which medieval people might 'define their class, power, monetary value', no less than their clothing or personal effects.[59]

Although Chaucer shows little interest in appellation, only giving the Reeve's horse a name, his list provides a reliable guide to understanding equine names as a whole. The division in naming can be read against precisely the same class distinctions that Chaucer adumbrates. It also presupposes that the destriers owned by emperors, kings, lords and knights should not be treated like ordinary workhorses and mounts; that is, it does not merely expose a disparity in naming, or between types of text, but betrays a sense that the horses associated with privileged social groups are a distinct order of creature. Indeed, some evidence suggests that elite groups did prefer names of this kind: in 1303 Richard of Gravesend, Bishop of London, owned horses named Skyppergrys (Grey-Skipper) and Rameseye (Ram's-eye), while Eraud de Ventadour, seigneur of Donzenac, and Sir Roger Salwayn of York left horses named Derer (Traveller) and Manley (Resolute) in their wills of 1365 and 1420.[60] It is not difficult to infer why horses of this kind might require specialised titles. Not only were destriers more valuable than carthorses and palfreys in financial terms, but they also possessed broader social value, on the one hand as extensions of their owner's identity, on the other as units of exchange. Several narrative and documentary sources make named horses tokens in military and diplomatic transactions: in 1388 the 'great horse' ('magnum equuum') Rocafranca (Frankish-Fortress) was presented by Amadeus VII, Count of Savoy, to the Duke of Burgundy, much as his fictional counterparts Tencendor and Broiefort were submitted to Charlemagne and Ogier by defeated knights.[61] Either way, the naming of destriers elevates them above plain mounts and drafts, much like the names given to

racehorses today. Once again, the socio-economic strands of medieval culture have a direct hand in creating divisions to which naming responds.

While much of this recalls dog-naming, horse-names also have quirks of their own. One of their most curious features is the fact that many consist of both a forename and surname. Representative are the horses purchased by Reymund de Burgh in 1340 on behalf of Edward III: among his acquisitions are Lyard de Burgh, Ferrant Makgibbyn, Soudan Roche, Sorel Borgh and Donnyng Cussak.[62] Later sources provide further examples: Bayard Nesfeld in the 1393 will of Johannes Fayrfax, Bayard Grenecobbe in the 1396 will of Thomas atte Wode, Liard de Watton in the 1380 will of Henricus Snayth, and Lyard Baraclough in the 1503 will of Sir Ranulphus Pigott of Clotherham.[63] Likewise, an inventory of the goods at Holt Castle in 1464 includes Sorel Prysse, Lyard Kesche, Lyard Hanmer and Bayard Thrope.[64] Although this convention seems to be confined to the British Isles, there is slight evidence of wider currency. The custom may be burlesqued in an anecdote Béroalde tells of Rabelais: the writer is supposed to have enrolled his horse at the Orange College of Breda under the name Doctor Joannes Cavallus (Dr John Horse), and paid for the animal to obtain its doctorate before the trick was uncovered.[65]

Even at first glance, these bipartite names further emphasise the proximity of horses to medieval human beings. It cannot be chance that the only animal to receive humanlike binomial names is the one most firmly integrated into medieval work, movement and warfare, and allegedly possessed of near-human sensitivity. This point is borne out further by the names themselves. Although

some convey other pieces of information, the majority signify either the breeder or trader of a horse, or the location
from which it originated, much as medieval anthroponyms
express familial or geographic provenance. Hence the Gray
Hodgeson that appears in Christoferus Aske's will of 1538
seems to take its name from its seller, much as the surnames
on Burgh's list record his status as buyer.[66] Correlatively, the
Black Prince's list includes the toponyms Bayard Lancastre,
Sorel Caunterbury, Bayard de Brucell (Bay of Brussells), Grisel de Luyton (Grey of Luton), and Morel de Paris, and the
1495 will of Johannes Hert, precentor of York Minster, refers
to Lyard Otterley.[67] Yet even while these designations are
directly imitative of human naming, they ultimately serve
their own purpose. They seem to encode the sale of the referent rather than simply stating its origin, commemorating
who bought them or where they were bought, much like a
modern-day receipt. As a result, they are a reminder of the
sway that commercial concerns hold over animal names,
even those that closely echo human naming conventions.

ALL THE BEASTS BY THEIR NAMES: CATS, ASSES AND OTHERS

Once we venture beyond horses and dogs towards other
species, zoonyms become thinner on the ground; they also
grow recognisably more stereotyped. Cats, for instance,
have highly conventionalised names, generally simple
diminutives or calling names. In English their usual name
is Gibbe, a pet-form of Gilbert or Guibert.[68] Although we
can infer that Malkin and Pusse were also commonplace,
Gibbe is by far the best attested. Hence Lydgate and Henryson include 'Gyb, the catte' and 'Gib Hunter our jolie cat'

in their translations of Aesop, while Skelton makes 'Gyb our cat savage' the murderer of his Philip Sparrow.[69] Further Gibbes are found in the ballads 'Ten Wives on their Husband's Ware' (c.1475) and 'Marriage of the Frogge and the Mouse' (c.1580), as well as Peele's *Edward I* (c.1590), Fulwell's *Like Will to Like* (c.1568), and *Gammer Gurton's Needle* (c.1562).[70] Inevitably, they also surface in witch-trials as 'spirit familiars': Gibbe was the 'great black cat' of Jennit Dibble, a widow of Knaresborough hanged in 1621.[71] The name seems to have developed its association with the species during the fourteenth century. In the English version of the *Roman de la Rose*, the liar Fals Semblant compares his 'bigilyng' to the ruses of 'Gibbe our cat', and in 1392 the name appears on the seal of the clerk Gilbert Stone as part of the motto 'GRET: WEL: GIBBE: OURE: CAT'.[72]

Other European languages take the same approach. In French, Raoul is a typical name for a 'gris chat' in the miracle play *Le Martyr de Saint Denis* (c.1500); the cat Tibaut from the Reynard-cycle might represent another convention, since his name reappears in a generalised sense in the original *Roman de la Rose* (c.1275) and in Rabelais's *Pantagruel* (c.1532).[73] In Old Irish, cat-names are even codified in law, with the treatise *Senchas Már* (c.900) citing Meoinne (Little-miaow) as an apt name for 'a pantry cat', Crúibne (Little-paw) for 'a cat of barn and mill', and Breoinne (Little-purr?) for a 'protecting' cat.[74] Sometimes feline appellatives are expressly identified as customary. The sixteenth-century lexicographer Anthoni Smyters includes the Dutch proper noun Min (Sweetheart, or Miaow) in his vocabulary of cat-related terms, and a note from Zurich in 1504 glosses Burrli (Furry) as 'Katzenname'.[75] This uniformity even seems to have crossed linguistic boundaries, given that the thirteenth-century French name Mite (Miaow) has later equivalents in German and the Baltic languages.[76] The normativity of these terms is further cemented by occasional departures from them. While different, more elaborate cat-names appear from time to time, they are invariably outlandish or given to creatures that are themselves emphatically abnormal. Such pointedly deviant names include Rabelais's Rodilardus (Fat-chewer), a gigantic 'devilkin with haywire hair' ('diableteau à poil follet'), and William Baldwin's talking cats Mousleer (Mouse-slayer), Titton-Tatton and Cachrat (Catch-rat) from the horror-satire *Beware the Cat*.[77] In fact, the same pattern is visible in cultures outside Europe. In China Wū yuán (Dark Plumpness) was the usual cat-name from at least the fourteenth century, appearing in the poetry of Liu Ji, an early Qing-era wall-hanging, and multiple later sources.[78]

It goes without saying that this homogeneity is markedly different from the varied and nuanced names given to dogs, and signals some obvious disparities between the two animals and their treatment. These perfunctory, mechanistic appellatives point to a creature only partly integrated into human activity. Although the choice of names implies some recognition of agency – Gibbe and Raoul are of course adapted human names, and most others seem to mimic the cat's 'voice' – their sameness suggests greater indifference and distance. All told, they place the cat on the fringes of domestic space, as an entity operating more or less autonomously, and requiring little in the way of linguistic contact or refined definition. This is not to say that medieval cats could never be objects of affection or esteem: a number of individual cats were demonstrably elevated

into companions, although these tended to receive unorthodox names that set them apart from other felines, such as Isabella d'Este's Martino, Joachim du Bellay's Belaud, or Pangur Bán (White Kneader?) at ninth-century Reichenau.[79] But the fact remains that the most widespread cat-names in the period put cats at a lesser level of contact with the human world than that enjoyed by dogs and horses.

The names given to exotic pets such as birds and primates exhibit much the same standardisation, although they do so for markedly different reasons. In French, monkeys were customarily called Bertrand or Robert according to the seventeenth-century philologist Ménage; in English, Martyn or Jacke were preferred terms, and were sufficiently clichéd by the fifteenth century to provide a visual pun in the arms of the Martyn family, and to expand into the pejorative term 'lacke a napes'.[80] The generic parrot-name Poll (from Mary) might also be medieval in origin: even though medieval parrots are typically identified by species alone, like Thomas de Saluces' 'trois perroquets' or Lyndsay's 'papyngo', the name had become proverbial by the late sixteenth century, when Jonson describes a character stricken with illness as 'poor Poll'.[81] The conventionalisation of these two sets of names is reminiscent of cat-names, but probably arises out of differing circumstances. Since parrots and monkeys would be imported as novelty status symbols for wealthy households, they were unlikely to be kept or encountered in large numbers, and would hardly require an extensive lexicon of appellatives. But they do at least share with cat-names a recognition of the creatures' intelligence, something encoded in their humanlike forms, and central to the animals' appeal as pets.

More complex is the set of names given to asses. To an extent, donkeys are also labelled much like cats: whenever they appear in medieval sources, they invariably possess one of a small number of rudimentary names. The richest testimony to this convention occurs in the unlikely context of scholastic philosophy, where the beasts are a longstanding academic in-joke.[82] The most common appellation here is Brunellus (Brownie). The name first occurs in the 1120s in Peter Abelard's bogus syllogism 'proving' that Socrates is a donkey, and it is later used in much the same way by Alain of Lille and Joannes Majoris, and by the authors of the *Summa sophisticorum elencorum* (*c*.1175) and *Failacie vindobonenses* (*c*.1175), among others.[83] It is also the name Nigel Wireker chooses for the protagonist of his wide-ranging academic satire *Speculum stultorum* (*c*.1190), where Brunellus is an ass ashamed of his short tail, who tours the universities of Europe to find a means of extending it.[84] Over the next four centuries logicians continue to evoke asses in their propositions, and in the process document more names for them. Hence Paul of Venice, Henry of Ghent and Albert of Saxony give us Favellus (Sandy-brown), while William of Sherwood mentions Morellus (Darkie), and Thomas Aquinas and Juan Dolz del Castellar refer to Grisellus (Grey).[85]

Given where they are preserved, the temptation might be to discount these labels as mere literary confections. Sometimes they undeniably appear to be little more than truisms. Wireker in particular seems to be responsible for popularising Brunellus in later sources: when Chaucer refers to 'Daun Burnel the Asse' in his *Nun's Priest's Tale*, and the Chester Cappers's play (*c*.1500) calls Balaam's ass 'Burnell', both are likely looking back to his *Speculum*.[86] Nonetheless, it is still fair to assume that these simple colour-names represent accepted designations for donkeys. Later evidence supports their basic currency: in Cervantes's *Don Quixote* (1605), for instance, Sancho Panza's long-suffering mount is dubbed El rucio (The dapple).[87] Indeed, like the grotesque cat-names, when other names are given to the creatures, they are either dubious or self-consciously ridiculous. In the latter category falls Carcophas (Load-carrier), a pretentious ass in *Ysengrimus*; in the former falls Tacor (Quiet), a donkey supposedly used by Frederick the Great to humiliate the city of Milan, by fixing 'a fig at the shameful parts of Tacor, and publicly forcing all the Milanese prisoners to pluck this fig with their teeth under pain of being hanged'.[88] Both suggest that donkeys would only be given more elaborate labels in jest.

Yet while ass-names mirror cat-names, and also show medieval culture defining lesser-valued organisms in dismissive, broad-brush terms, they carry their own implications. Particularly remarkable is their frequent application to horses. Although posterity has linked the fourteenth-century philosopher John Buridan with asses, he generally preferred to evoke named *equi* instead of *asini* in his work: his *Sophisms* explicitly define Brunellus, Morellus, and Favellus as 'good horses' when reflecting on exchange and equivalence.[89] The same names are also allocated to horses by Ockham, Dorp, Mercarius and De Soto.[90] Likewise, when Gervais de Bus borrowed the name Favellus for his scathing satire *Roman de Fauvel* (1314), he understood it as a horse-name, giving it to the 'noble cheval' whose talent for securing homage produced the phrases 'torcher Fauvel' and 'curry Favel'.[91] Other sources yield still more horses by these names: Grise, Morele and Fauvel are coupling stallions and mares in the *Roman de la Rose*, ard the gift-horses of the Black Prince include beasts named Morel, Grisel and Gris; in the *Alliterative Morte Arthur* (*c*.1375) Sir Florent likewise rides 'Fawnell of Friseland'.[82] Sometimes it is unclear which creature these names might denote. A particularly grotesque instance occurs in a thirteenth-century fabliau, in which a bashful new wife is given the coceword 'feed oats to Morel' ('donne a Morel de l'avaine') tc signal that she wants sex; after her appetite starts to tire her husband, he cools her ardour by giving her 'bran instead of oats' ('bren en leu d'aveinne') – that is, shitting on her rather than ejaculating.[83] Although hardly its central point, the piece never specifies what Morel might mean for its characters, and its open-endedness again signals the flexibility of the name. These confusions are perhaps only logical, given that asses and workhorses would perform identical roles in the same rural settings; but their interchangeability again spotlights the power of function over identity, to the extent that it can compromise the lines dividing species.

These same pressures are also perceptible in other sets of names. Some designations in fact show themselves capable of impressive leaps between disparate types of animal. Perhaps more striking than ass-names are the appellations given to hawks and other birds of prey. Many names of hunting-birds recall those of hunting-dogs. Several seem designed to evoke the origins of their bearers, much as Biondo claims that Italian dogs might 'also derive their name from their country, so that one born among the Britons is called Britannus, among the French Gallus, and so on'.[94] Hence Henry III owned a hawk named

Pilgrim and a goshawk named Lespanyol (Spaniard), the first probably imported from the Holy Land and the second from the Iberian peninsula.[95] Others recall the colourfully metaphoric names typical of hound-naming: such doglike names include those assigned to King John's gyrfalcon Gibbun (Hunchback), Henry III's hawk Blakemanne (Blackman), and the 'haggard falcon' Stella (Star) owned by Lord Henry Berkeley in the 1580s.[96] There are in fact several points at which dog-names and hawk-names converge, or where the line between them is otherwise blurred: Henry III's gyrfalcon Blanchpenny (Silver-penny) looks forward to the Tudor dog-names Silver and Sixpence, and Conrad Gessner and the *Master of Game* include Falco and Fawcon among the recommended names for greyhounds.[97] It is not too much of a stretch to see here the same conflation glimpsed in ass-names and horse-names. Given that both hawks and hounds were deployed in the pursuit of game, and that both were owned by the same social groups, the analogies are unlikely to be accidental.[98]

The same point can be extended further still by looking to the ox, although the conventions around this creature prove especially difficult to interpret. Mainly this is because oxen leave only slight traces: while the Jacobean zoologist Edward Topsell assures us that 'every man hath a proper and peculiar name for his Dog, as well as for his Oxe', he promptly undermines this claim offering no names for oxen, despite quoting fifteen dog-names from Biondo and Gessner.[99] This startling lack of reference to such a commonplace creature implies a generally neutral attitude towards it, one that prevented the ox from being taken up by any particular literary or economic discourse: being less prestigious than the horse, but less obviously comedic than the ass, it is probable that authors simply could not find useful meanings in the ox to exploit. Indeed, it is possible that the animals were not given unique identifiers at all. Early modern sources sometimes point in this direction: one of the stories associated with Baron Munchausen states that only John Mowmowsky, the lead ox that pulled the baron's carriage, had his own name, while 'the rest were called Jacks in general, but not dignified by any particular denomination'.[100] Oxen are also routinely left unnamed in wills and other inventories: the 1461 will of Ricardus de Ley lists his horse as Bosse but identifies his ox only as ʿbuculum', and no names are assigned to the two oxen listed among the assets of Petrocino Casalesco, Archbishop of Ravenna, at the time of his death in 1369.[101]

On balance, however, sources suggest that medieval oxen would usually be given labels of their own, like their ancestors on the Knossos tablets, even if we cannot always determine what they were. Hence the plough-team driven by Piers Plowman in Langland's poem of the same name consists of 'foure grete oxen' Luk, Mark, Matthew and Johan; while these allegorical names are unlikely to reflect real-world appellations, they do at least suggest that each ox would have an individual designation.[102] Other sources confirm this point, even though they are again unlikely to reflect real-life praxis. Named oxen include Harri, four-horned ox of the Icelandic trader Ólafur Höskuldsson in the *Laxdœla saga* (*c*.1200), Pieter Osse (Peter Ox) in a Dutch burlesque sermon of *c*.1550, and Vehemot (Behemoth), the ox who causes earthquakes in a snippet of fourteenth-century Jewish folklore.[103] Perhaps closer to reality are Cain's plough-team in the Towneley play *The Killing of Abel*, or Rudd and Goore from the 'Balade of the Plough' (*c*.1500), even though this second text seems to be an elaborate innuendo, emphasising the plough's power to 'dryve in, theghe the lande were roughe'.[104] If these examples reflect actual conventions, then ox-names were, like ass-names, indistinguishable from the names given to workhorses. One of Cain's steers has the common ass/horse-name Morell, and another Rudd appears among the horses sold by Richard of Gravesend in 1303.[105] Once again, function proves a vital determinant of medieval naming, at times overriding species distinctions.

Yet while most of the evidence points to oxen having individual names, there are cases in which other animals were treated in sweeping terms. This is particularly true of livestock, whose names sometimes function more like mass than proper nouns. While individual cattle show up in wills from time to time, such as Sourell, the cow left in 1551 by John Watson, vicar of Mekle Usburne, their names are often more generic than specific.[106] Something of this tendency can be seen in the 1235 will of Guillelmus Petrus de Bolhaco, a dairy farmer near the Cistercian abbey of Grandselve in the county of Toulouse. Guillelmus shows a striking vacillation between levels of meaning when cataloguing his small herd. Although each cow has her own given name, such as Nacoia (Grumpy), Mansa (Meek) and Amorosa (Affectionate), several are labelled identically: no fewer than three are called Cirgua (Wander).[107] Other cow-names also seem intended to denote groups rather than single entities. A similar case is Bouchoda, which appears in fourteenth-century wills from Saint-Just, Bellegarde and

Saint-Etienne as a given name for a cow, but probably means something like 'beef cattle'.[108]

While these expansive names are relatively unusual, their collective sensibility is not. On the whole, there are far fewer reliable names for livestock and poultry in the period than there are for other domesticated species. A couple do occur. Chaucer's widow in the *Nun's Priest's Tale* owns a ewe named Malle (Maudy), and his Wife of Bath a ram called Wilkyn (Willy); this second name seems conventional, since it is also figuratively applied to pile-driving equipment, such as 'the ghynne callyd the Wilkynn Ramme of bras' used at London bridge in the 1460s.[109] Likewise, the *Towneley Second Shepherd's Play* (*c*.1450) and *Tournament of Tottenham* (*c*.1440) mention hens called Copyle and Coppeld, both perhaps onomatopoeic renderings of the bird's characteristic 'kakyls'.[110] A piece of Tudor underworld slang might preserve two traditional names for geese: 'Roger' and 'Tyb of the buttery' are supposed to have been cant terms for these birds, whose noisy territorialism was obviously feared by thieves and beggars.[111] Mostly, however, livestock and poultry are named for symbolic and mythopoetic reasons: examples include the primordial cow Auðhumla, the fearsome warrior-cow Síbilja in *Ragnars saga* (*c*.1300), and the cocks Fjalarr (Concealer) and Gullinkambi (Golden-comb) whose crowing announces the onset of Ragnarök.[112] Otherwise, they tend to receive names for the familiar humorous ends. Aside from the cast of *Ysengrimus*, two cases in point are the pig Groignet (Grunter) in Claude de Pontoux's absurd 1571 elegy, and the hog Preecker (Preacher) in a farce from Haarlem.[113] Preecker's name in particular is simply a pretext for comic confusion, sparking panic when a Dominican friar overhears his owners making plans to 'slit the throat of our Preacher' ('onsen preecker den halsch afsteecken').[114] The general scarcity of these names points to their greater degree of conventionalisation, and shows the records taking little interest in their referents as singular beings. Either way, it signals that medieval culture conceived these creatures as members of a group first and foremost, and saw little need to allocate them specialised appellations, or even discuss them as individuals at all.

Nevertheless, the rarity of a zoonym might carry other meanings, and indicate quite different attitudes towards the species associated with it. There are a few names whose anomalousness seems to be the entire point, and whose own strangeness marks a creature or the circumstances of naming as odd in some way. These wilfully absurd names might also be used for comedic purposes: this is clearly true of the names of the wolves Septengula Nipig (Seven-throated Pincher), Gulpa Gehenna Minor (Gulping Little Hellfire) and Turgius Ingens Mantica (Bloated Immense Feed-bag) in *Ysengrimus*, where the joke is not only the overblown character of the names themselves, but the fact that they are given to beasts who do not normally have or need them.[115] At other times, however, they might be used to highlight the monstrosity of creatures, indicating that they have departed from natural bounds in some way. This appears to be case for the real-life wolf Coutaut (Stump-tail), leader of a pack that attacked and ate fourteen Parisians in 1439: according to one witness, Coutaut attained the notoriety 'of a bandit of the greenwood or a cruel captain, for one would say to people heading out to the fields: "Beware of Coutaut"'.[116] References to whales also periodically take the form much of a stretch to see them falling into much the same pattern Edmund Leach identifies when thinking about which animal-words are used for endearments and which for insults: like Leach's model, in which the values of 'bunny' and 'bitch' are determined by the creatures nearness to the human home, animal names also serve to assert the focal position of the human being – they are anthropocentric in the strictest sense of the term.[126] All told, they show how the human being's presumed centrality is another potent element in organising the animal world, much as it was for Isidore in his remarks on canine 'wisdom' and equine sensitivity. But they also raise interesting questions about how medieval culture maintained this structure, and preserved the pivotal status of the human, even wher granting identities to inhuman beasts. Our next, final chapter will turn to this issue.

CHAPTER 5

IMPROPER NOUNS:
HUMAN AND ANIMAL NAMES

WHILE WAR AND ANIMALS are favourite themes in medieval poetry, the two are not often brought into conjunction. An exception, however, is a piece written in 1230 by the Italian-born knight, diplomat and *chanteor* Philippe of Novara. Philippe's work is equally notable for its content and for the circumstances in which it was composed. Between 1219 and 1243, Philippe witnessed escalating tensions between his patron John of Ibelin, lord of Beirut, and Emperor Frederick II as the two tussled over Cyprus and Jerusalem, territories that John effectively controlled as regent to the young king Henry I. Tensions boiled over in 1229 when three of the five lords backed by Frederick, and known as the 'five props of Cyprus' ('cinq baus de Chypre'), abducted the twelve-year-old Henry and barricaded themselves in Deudamor, now St Helion Castle, in the Kyrenia mountains. After a year-long siege they surrendered to John, who used the opportunity to sue for peace on his terms. However, Philippe refused to support any treaty, being unable to forgive the 'evils and outrages' ('maus et otrages') the *baus* had committed over the previous few years.[1]

In order to register his disgust, but without endangering John's precarious peace, Philippe composed a new *branche*

of the fashionable stories of Reynard the Fox.[2] In Bossuat's estimation, the piece shows thorough knowledge of the cycle, managing to weave in most of its 'several named beasts' ('nouma bestes plusors').[3] However, beneath its playful knockabout, Philippe embedded a secret message: when he came to transcribe the poem in later life as part of his *Mémoires*, after his enemies were either dead or disgraced, he also provided a key to its contents. As he explains, 'all the beasts that are on the side of Yzengrin' ('toutes ces bestes sont de la partie d'Yzengrin') in fact represent Philippe, his benefactor and friends: John and his children are the wolf Yzengrin and his cubs, Sir Anceau de Bries is Bruin the bear, and Philippe himself Chanteclere the cock. The *baus* on the other hand are identified with 'those beasts on the side of Reynard in the same stories' ('celes bestes sont de la partie de Renart au roumans meïsmes'): Aimery Barlais is the fox himself, Amaury de Bethsan is Grimbert the badger, and Hugues de Giblet is Martin the monkey.[4]

Philippe does not record the consequences of this inflammatory pastiche, although notes that the subsequent treachery of his enemies handsomely justified its invective. He states with grim satisfaction that he had 'well foretold and outlined in the *branche* of Renart what they did afterward'.[5] But one point that stands out from this affair is the striking use that Philippe makes of the period's most famous set of zoonyms. Approached in one way, his appropriation of the names Reynard, Grimbert and the others seems to confirm conventional wisdom about medieval attitudes towards animal and human identities, in that its wilful confusion of the two is a deliberate perversion of normal practice. Not only was the code forced on Philippe by circumstances outside his control, but its intent is clearly a subversive one: as Fukumoto observes, in Philippe's hands the Reynard tradition 'goes quite beyond the remit of satire' and is turned into 'an instrument of *ad hominem* attack'.[6] In other words, the projection of one sphere on to the other is by design an outrageous act, one mobilised against Philippe's sworn enemies. His work then seems to recognise that there should normally be a distinction between the names given to animals and those given to human beings, since it aggressively overturns such a convention.

The idea that medieval culture did its utmost to draw a line between human and animal names, as a means of preserving the primacy of the human being, is widespread in scholarship. Its foundational statement appears in the work of Claude Lévi-Strauss in the 1960s. Discussing the implicit structures that govern animal-naming, Lévi-Strauss argues that only animals such as birds might be given human names, since they safely occupy their own separate 'metaphoric' sphere; conversely, beasts forming 'part of human society' such as dogs, horses and cattle tend to receive distinctive markers 'rarely borne by ordinary human beings'.[7] Much the same assessment has been put forward by Robert Bartlett, Jeffrey Jerome Cohen and Keith Thomas, who agree that medieval animals were 'usually given names that are distinct from those given to human beings' or 'seldom carried the same appellations used among humans', in order to avoid 'any risk of confusion between animal and human'; Dorothy Yamamoto likewise grounds her analysis of human and natural identities on Lévi-Strauss's claims.[8] Even Stephen Wilson, who finds copious evidence of human-based animal names in Old French, concludes that this approach

is peculiar to the language and not shared by other medieval cultures to a significant degree.[9]

Of course, at a simple factual level, there are some immediate problems with this generalisation. Despite enjoying the weight of Lévi-Strauss's authority, the evidence is squarely against it. We have already encountered numerous breaches of this supposed rule, many of which rank among the best attested names in the period: the cat-names Gibbe and Raoul, the dog-names Colle, Goby and Hog, the horse-names Scot and Gyll, the goose-name Tyb, and the sheep-names Malle and Wilkin. Nor are these choices solely dictated by custom: there are numerous more isolated instances, such as Lord Berkeley's 'haggard falcon' Kate in the 1580s, Johannes Bery's horse Aylstan (Athelstan) in his 1375 will, the deer Wyl Bucke in a poem of *c.*1520, the 'ambling horse' Symon in the 1524 will of John Brent, and Pettiwatte (Little-Walter), Dow (Ralphy) and Huwet (Hugh) among the Black Prince's gift-horses.[10] In fact, the widespread application of anthroponyms to animals did not escape the notice of early commentators. Writing in the seventeenth century, Gilles Ménage reflects that 'we have given an infinite number of human names to animals', and is able to assemble a formidable list of examples from French: Janne for a goat, Jacquet for a squirrel, Sansonnet for a blackbird, Colas for a crow, and so on.[11] In short, it barely needs stating that anthroponyms were applied to a wide range of animals in the period, despite its assurance in the God-given supremacy of the human being.

However, beyond its simple failure to reflect the realities of medieval culture, the assumption that a taboo governed zoonyms also presents more serious problems.

Something of this can be seen in Philippe's usage of the Reynard characters. While his work supports these ideas to a degree, Philippe clearly regards any boundary between naming systems as permeable and manipulable rather than inviolable: although he presents his veiled attack as a workaround forced on him against his wishes, he evidently wrote in expectation that his code would be cracked by an attentive reader, and that human referents might be recognised in these non-human names. But more striking is the fact that his evocation of Reynard is largely indifferent to the accepted hierarchy between human and animal. Stinging though his satire is, it does not enlist the names only for purposes of slander: while some are intended to insult the *baus*, the identities of Philippe's friends and patron are also hidden in others, along with that of the author himself. In other words, it is not the case that confusing animal and human nomenclature serves only to defame and degrade. Philippe's Reynardian pastiche shows that relaxing this distinction was not merely permissible, but that it could serve multiple ends. The situation is evidently less predictable than received wisdom acknowledges.

As a result, Philippe's work allows us to steer enquiry away from simply assessing the validity of Lévi-Strauss's position, and towards some more interesting questions. Instead of asking whether human and animal identities could be merged, it allows us to ask why they might be. What circumstances allowed this intermixing to occur? What effects might it produce? Which names or types of names could travel across the human/animal boundary? Which animals received human appellations? But over and above these questions, it also compels us to consider a further point, and

think about how medieval language coped with this potential erosion of identities and species. In short, re-examining the use of human names allows us to address a range of questions that the taboo theory pushes aside. Indeed, as we shall see, when taboo-like mechanisms do impact on zoonyms, they often prove more generative than repressive.

But before exploring these questions, it is worth addressing a further point of interest in human-derived names – their curious ability to change into common nouns over time. Many of the terms we still use today are in fact medieval animal names that underwent this transition. Perhaps the clearest instance is the word 'robin'. Our contemporary term, derived from a pet-form of Robert, seems to have overtaken the earlier 'redbrest' around *c.*1520, when it first appears as a standalone word in the Chaucerian pastiche *Parlyament of Birds*.[12] Before this point, a number of sources show its currency as a fanciful appellation for the bird, including 'Robert redbrest' in an earlier *Parliament of Birds* (*c.*1440), 'robynet redbrest' in a fifteenth-century wordlist, and 'a byrde called Robyn redbrest' in Elyot's *Dictionary* (1538); 'Robin red brest' is also the solution to a popular Tudor riddle beginning 'I am cald by the name of man'.[13] Magpie evidently charted a similar journey. Early references imply that Magge (Maggy) was a standard medieval name for a chattering bird: in his *Tale of Jonathas* (*c.*1420), Hoccleve frets that hostile readers might liken him to 'Magge the good kow [chough]', and the name recurs in the idiom 'maggetales' or 'magel tale', used against heretics by Nicholas Love in *c.*1409 and against Arthurian legend by John Trevisa in *c.*1387.[14] Over the next few centuries it develops its current association with the species *Pica pica*, known in Middle English as the 'pye'. The two terms appear in various combinations, including 'maggot-a-pie' and 'magget the pie', before finally consolidating as 'magpy' around the time of the tract *Mar-Martine* (1589).[15] Jackdaw seems to have taken a similar course. It is first recorded in its current form in Rastell's *Interlude of the Four Elements* (1520), although might be implicit in the interlinked treatises *Jack Upland* and *Reply of Friar Daw* (*c*.1390).[16] Either way, the term is likely a compound similar to magpie, knitting together the earlier species-name 'dawe' and an anthroponym popularly given to the bird.

Beyond these avian names, other terms in present-day English have clearly travelled down the same track. Comparable are the related terms 'dobbin', first attested as a generic horse-name in *c*.1598, and 'hobbyhorse', documented as a child's toy from 1568.[17] Both words are derivatives of Hobbe (Robby), a name customarily given to ponies in the fourteenth and fifteenth centuries. Hence the Black Prince made a gift of 'Lyard Hobyn' to a godson in 1352, while the 1458 will of John Wrygh of Wickham Skeith also lists a horse named 'Hobbe'.[18] Between these two dates, the term had already started to function as a general term for a small mount: in the *Laud Troy Book* (*c*.1400), the Grecian cavalry are said to consist of 'hoby, stede, and gode rounsi', and the 1420 will of Sir Roger Salwayn pledges a nameless 'hoby' to the son of Sir Robert Shottesbroke.[19] 'Bunny' might likewise have developed out of the forename Bunne.[20] Before taking on its modern meaning around *c*.1620, when the ballad 'The Hunting of the Conney' uses it to describe a rabbit, it is a common name for several small pets: 'little pretie Bun' is a runaway squirrel in a story told by Thomas Churchyard in 1587, and witch-trial records mention a cat, puppy and toad

by the name.[21] There are a few more terms besides whose etymologies are otherwise difficult to explain. Keith Briggs speculates that 'wolverine' might show analogous development out of the personal name Wulfram, and 'willock', first recorded by the navigator Jonas Poole in 1604, seems to have grown out of a popular tendency to dub seabirds 'Willie'.[22] In each of these cases our own language gives witness to medieval naming convention, showing its strange habit of turning human names into collective nouns for animals.

As well as these terms still with us today, there are numerous less-enduring examples.[23] An especially curious instance is Watte (Walter), which manages to attach itself to two distinct species in the late Middle Ages. In the 1380s, Chaucer treats it as a standard name for a jay: he compares the unlettered Summoner to a babbling 'jay [that] kan clepen "Watte" as wel as kan the pope', no doubt having in mind a caged bird trained to repeat its name.[24] Around the same date the name is also used as a synonym for jays in general: the *c*.1440 *Parliament of Birds* introduces the 'rusti chateryng of þe iay' with the lines 'þus watte gan syngyn in his lay', and in *c*.1381 Gower glosses the Latin *graculus avis* with the explanation 'in English "jay", commonly called "Watte"' ('anglice Gay, qui vulgariter vocatur Watte').[25] A little later Watte gains the same status in relation to hares. In the lyric *Mourning of the Hunted Hare* (*c*.1475), a huntsman addresses his eponymous quarry with the statement 'Aryse upe, Watte, and go forthe'.[26] Other sources treat it in a more generalised sense: another lyric from *c*.1500 describes a schoolboy wishing that his 'master were a watt / And my boke a wyld catt', and the henpecked narrator of *The Complaynte of them that ben to late maryed* (*c*.1505) compares his own 'dolours and crayntes' to those of a 'wat after the hounde'.[27] Alongside these relatively well-documented names, early modern witnesses contain a number of other terms that can be justly considered results of the same process. When, for example, a 1577 indenture for a fisherman's apprentice refers to eel-traps as 'grygge wieles', or a 1589 dictionary defines 'a shorte legged henne' as 'a Grigge', both suggest earlier usage of Gregory in its pet-form to denote these animals.[28] The wide distribution of 'jack' as a masculine particle might tell a similar story: we find 'jack-dog' in *c*.1597, 'Jack Herring' in 1598, 'jack-snipe' in 1664, 'Jack curlew' in 1676, 'Jack Merlin', 'Jack Hobby', 'Jack Castrell [Kestrel]' and 'Jack Hare' in 1686, and 'jackass' in 1695, each of which might also build on medieval practice.[29] Further cases might be 'tom tit', first recorded in a pastoral by Mildmay Fane from *c*.1649, and 'Gill-hooter', a folk-name for a grey owl noted by Francis Willughby in 1676, apparently in recognition of the bird's 'strong cry' ('forte ulula').[30] All these examples might also look back to medieval customs, representing the end-point of the same expansion Magge, Robin and Hobbe underwent. There are also suggestions of similar processes in other European languages. In French, Ménage theorises that the words *perroquet* (parrot), *matou* (tomcat) and *marcassin* (boar) evolved out of the traditional appellatives Pierre, Marcolf and Marc.[31]

On the one hand, the tendency of human-derived names to behave in this way underscores their pervasiveness: it goes without saying that Hobbe and Magge must have been widely used and highly recognisable to become so firmly anchored to their species. But it is not only the fact of their existence that makes these names significant; equally important is what they tell us about animal-naming

in general. Their semantic widening highlights one of the key questions that hangs over zoonyms, how they managed to preserve the integrity of the human/animal divide even when testing it. In particular, their slipperiness reminds us of the implicit drift towards the generic in all animal names. Their development over time is clearly rooted in a sense that their referents are basically metonymic and exemplary, representing the larger groups of which they are part, rather than being unique subjects in their own right. The expansion of Jack, Hobbe and Robin into common nouns would scarcely be possible if their objects were not understood as typifying and denoting their species, gender or order of creature from the first: to echo Derrida, and Bentham before him, they show language entering a 'general singular' mode when describing animals, making each 'represent, like an ambassador' their 'species ... genus or kingdom' even while treating it as '*this* irreplaceable living being'.[32] As a consequence, they make clear that naming does not need to forbid traffic across the border between human and animal, as Lévi-Strauss and his followers assume. Its implicit structures already offer adequate protection against attrition of this boundary, by giving animals an identity conspicuously different from that enjoyed by human beings. Indeed, the playfulness of the names shows the security of this distinction, as they approach it with greater whimsy than anxiety.

Nonetheless, these issues are not the only oddities that anthroponyms throw up. A further puzzle is exactly why some of these creatures have been given names at all, let alone names drawn from the human sphere. It stands to reason that pets or working animals would receive names of this kind, given their entanglement in the emotional, domestic or professional lives of their owners. The purpose in naming a hare, robin or owl, however, is not so easy to grasp. After all, creatures of this kind are remote from human influence, inhabiting the wild places beyond the household, park or farmyard. In short, they are not obvious targets for anthropomorphism.

One text that might explain their logic is the peculiar thirteenth-century poem 'Les noms de un leure en engleis' ('The Names of a Hare in English'). Described by its Victorian editors as 'a very curious composition', this poem shows how popular belief might be a further factor in shaping linguistic practice.[33] It outlines the measures that any 'mon þat þe hare imet' must undertake in order to ward off the misfortune the creature brings with it. First, he must drop any item he is carrying, and bless himself with an elbow, before reciting an 'oreisoun … in þe worshipe of þe hare'; once this petition is complete, 'þenne miȝte þou wenden forþ / Est and west and souþ and norþ' without further worry. The most sustained part of the poem is the orison itself, which relates some eighty alternative designations for the hare: these epithets range from the abusive 'euele imet' (evil-met) and 'frendlese' (friendless), to the descriptive 'gobidich' (go-by-ditch) and 'deuhoppere' (dew-hopper), to the cryptic 'babbart' and 'momelart'. The final few labels make clear what motivates this bizarre catalogue:

> þe hert wiþ þe leþerene hornes;
> þe der þa woneþ in þe cornes;
> þe der þat alle men scornes;
> þe der þat nomon ne dar nemmen.[34]

> (The hart with the leather horns;
> The beast that dances in the corn;
> The beast that all men scorn;
> The beast that no man dares name.)

The text therefore seems to be describing a kind of superstition around the hare's regular name. Its cascade of colourful descriptions is prompted by a sense that some malign power adheres to the word 'hare' itself, and that this might be thwarted by using elaborate metaphors in its place, much as the Proto-Germanic *bero* ('brown thing', or 'wild beast') is thought to have displaced an older, loaded term for 'bear'.[35] Whether it is treating the idea facetiously or in earnest, the poem's synonyms conform to the anthropological definition of taboo: they are at root a 'restrictive behaviour' intended to effect 'protection of individuals who are in danger' by avoiding this inauspicious word.[36]

While Watte does not appear among these euphemisms and dysphemisms, it probably developed under similar conditions, as a benign equivalent for an ill-favoured term. It is certainly true that the hare retains its unlucky reputation throughout the medieval period and beyond. In *Wynnere and Wastoure* (*c*.1370), the image of 'hares appon herthestones' opens the sequence of disruptions portending 'dredfull Domesdaye', and in *c*.1400 John Trevisa describes 'olde wyfes' disguising themselves as hares through 'craft of nygramauncie' and stealing their neighbours' milk.[37] Writing in 1456, Johannes Hartlieb mentions similar beliefs, inveighing against the conviction that 'when someone encounters a hare that is bad luck', and one of the English redactions of *Mandeville's Travels* (*c*.1400) likewise holds that encountering a hare 'first at morwe' is 'full evill meetynge'.[38] The same idea also appears in quasi-medicalised form. The hare's proverbial habit of turning 'masid', 'mad' or 'brayn-les' in March gives rise to a related belief that its meat can transmit mental illness: Andrew Boorde warns that 'hares flesshe ... doth ingender melancoly humours', and Burton states that its 'black meat ... causeth fearful dreams'.[39]

These connotations are not unique to the hare, but are shared by many of the other wild animals who receive popular appellations. The magpie is also considered an omen of 'some evil before us', as the Scottish minister Robert Wodrow writes in the seventeenth century.[40] It is for this reason that its collective noun in Middle English is 'a tygendis of pyes', most likely a corruption of 'tidings', and that the *Gospel of the Distaffs* (1480) claims that hearing a magpie chattering on one's roof 'is the sign of bad news to come'.[41] Macbeth similarly includes 'maggot-pies' among the 'augurs' that promise 'blood will have blood', and Bruegel depicts one of the birds perching ominously on a gibbet in his *De ekster op de galg* (c.1568).[42] The jay and rabbit also carry similar associations. In the sixteenth century, the Swiss reformer Rudolf Gwalther interprets 'infernall iayes' as embodiments of 'the affections and suggestions of sathan', and later antiquarians note a longstanding belief that rabbits are signs of impending death.[43] The connections between owls and 'spiritual uncleanness' are likewise well-attested in literary and visual sources.[44]

Although it would be rash to read every name of this kind in such terms, the baleful influence that folklore often assigns to wild creatures may have led to similar reluctance to speak them directly; this hesitance in turn might

account for the emergence of such alternative designations as Bunne or Watte. It might even explain the nature of the names themselves. The fact that these names tend to be humanlike suggest that their intention is to appease their recipient in some way, treating them as a notional equal, much as the hare should be shown 'wel goed devosion'. In fact, comparable habits were still being observed well into the twentieth century: in the 1950s similar measures are recorded on the island of Portland in Dorset, where rabbits were supposedly called 'Wilfreds' to guard against bad luck, and Frazer discusses analogous practices among the fishing communities of the Moray Firth.[45] In short, evidence suggests that names such as Watte and Maggot might well be substitutive at root, arising out of popular taboos around their referents.

If this hypothesis is accepted, then it carries implications for naming as a whole, and the relationships it might express. In particular, it complicates the emotional aspect of naming considerably. The temptation is of course to assume that all names are born out of affection. This is undeniably true in numerous cases: from Zabot to Curribus and Pangur Bán, many animals have clearly entered the records because of the special esteem in which their owners held them. However, the folk-names given to the hare and other creatures hint at a more complex picture. Impulses such as fear, suspicion or hostility might just as easily lead to appellatives being created for non-human entities. In this respect, the folk-names chime with other names we have seen elsewhere, such as those given to man-eating wolves or destructive whales. Even hound-names and pet-names can show this wide spectrum of affect; for every Bo or Sweetlips there is a name denoting disgust or irritation. The *Master of Game* list finds place for Dredefull, Filthe, Oribull and Crab (Bitter apple), the last of which is explained by Shakespeare's Lance as a fit name for 'the sourest-natured dog that lives'.[46] Biondo also mentions owning a bitch called Furia (Fury), named for her irritable disposition, and a 'herd of dog-names' ('meenigte Hondenaamen') in an early modern Dutch satire includes Grypaart (Grabber), Dikkop (Thickhead) and Schuddegat (Twitchy-arsehole).[47] In the 1620s, Thomas Fairfax composed a memorial verse to 'ould Fough [Yuk]; my Grandam's farting dogg'.[48] Ultimately, names such as these caution us against joining appellation to one type of emotion alone. They recall Theodore Zeldin's claim that domestication was a pivotal moment in the history of emotion, one that changed human beings as much as animals, although in multiple and contradictory ways.[49]

A further and no less suggestive dimension opens up when we consider which human names are given to non-human creatures. It should be clear from the foregoing that the corpus of human-derived names is relatively uniform; it was not the case that any anthroponym could be transferred to an animal, since only names of a certain type make this leap. Specifically, most of the recorded examples are hypocoristic or pet-forms of proper nouns: Gybbe comes from Gilbert, Magge from Margaret, Dawe from Radolph, Watte from Walter, Gyll from Juliane, and so on. It has long been recognised that names of this kind were primarily associated with the peasantry in the Middle Ages. Beginning with the work of Lower and Bardsley in the late nineteenth century, the connection between these 'nick forms' and the 'plebeian' or 'lower classes' has often been noted.[50]

Literary sources in particular make frequent use of them to represent this social group, and the boorishness and lack of sophistication it was thought to embody. Two early examples are the 'Satire on the Consistory Courts' (*c.*1300) and 'Lutel Soth Sarmun' (*c.*1250): in the former the narrator describes the 'lewed' girls he has seduced as 'Magge ant Malle', while the latter rails against 'lechurs and horlinges' named 'Malekyn', 'wilekyn', 'Robyn' and 'Gilot'.[51] In the fourteenth century, the same names resurface in Langland's *Piers Plowman*, where Watte the Warner, Hikke the Hakeneyman and Dawe the Dykere make up a band of drunks.[52] They also occur in accounts of the English Rising of 1381: various Latin sources caricature the agitators with such emblematic figures as Iak Shepe, Hobbe Carter and Thom Myllere.[53]

In fact, so unmistakable is the similarity between animal names and these stereotypically 'plebeian' names that some medieval authors self-consciously exploit it. For instance, when John Gower's *Visio Anglie* reimagines the 1381 Rising as a stampede of rebellious beasts, he emphasises the confusion of animal and human by giving the perpetrators names that might pertain to either: Watte, Gibbe, Hykke, Colle, Wille, Dawe and Hobbe all feature among his bestialised rioters. A similar tack is adopted by the *Second Shepherd's Play* from the fifteenth-century Wakefield Corpus Christi cycle. Here the three shepherds, who eventually find themselves among the animals at Christ's manger, and who mistake a stolen lamb for a human infant on the way, are also pointedly given names that place them in both the animal and human worlds: they refer to one another as Coll, Gib and Daw.[54] In either case, the duality of these names is used to summon two sets of associations at once.

Nonetheless, despite the close alignment between animal-naming and peasant-naming, class is not the only social category to touch on zoonyms. Although they are not personal names in quite the same sense, there is a small but important subset that calls on human racial categories. Several such names appear in the *Master of Game* list: Jewe, Turke, Sowdan (Sultan) and Saresyn (Saracen) are among the author's recommendations. Most European languages have equivalents of at least one of these labels: Turcus (Turk) is one of Conrad Gessner's dog-names, and Soldan seems to have been a common canine name in Danish from an early date.[55] Türgk and Soldan are also listed at Zurich in 1504, along with the comparable Mörli (Little-Moor).[56] Appellations in this vein are also given to animals other than hounds. Blakemanne (Blackman) was one of Henry III's hawks, and Sareson (Saracen) was among the nine horses bequeathed in 1495 by Johannes Hert, precentor of York Minster.[57] Likewise, the horse whose hide is used to chastise an unruly wife in a Dutch farce of *c*.1525 is called Moorken (Little-Moor).[58] But the most widespread of these names is Morell, Morrel or Morellus, recorded in English, French, Latin and other languages from the thirteenth century as a proper noun for a horse or donkey. Morellus is also profoundly racialised: it is likely derived from the late classical 'maurus' or 'Moor', a term originally applied to the inhabitants of the African province of Mauretania, but later expanded to encompass the Muslim populations of the southern Mediterranean.[59]

Names such as these are difficult to parse, and need to be approached with a degree of care. It would of course be unwise to project contemporary sensitivities on to medieval

culture in a purely reflexive manner; doing so brings with it the attendant danger of forgetting that our own conceptions of race are historically situated, as writers such as Memmi and Dyer have taken pains to show.[60] It is also true that the exact intention of these names is sometimes hard to judge. Although they are probably meant to signify the coloration of an animal, evoking the skin-tones typically found in the Arabian peninsula and northern Africa, other possible meanings remain: an early French dictionary claims that Turc was traditionally used 'when speaking of a strong dog' ('en parlent d'un fort chien') rather than a dark-coated one.[61] However, despite these caveats, it cannot be denied that names such as these look forward to the racialised culture of more recent centuries, in ways that recall Geraldine Heng's remarks on medieval race.[62] In fact, giving animals names that evoke non-European ethnic groups anticipates some of the more disturbing longer-term trends in zoonyms. It looks forward to analogous patterns in the Georgian period. The fashion during the long eighteenth century was for classically derived names. Such conventions are vividly evoked by an anonymous author in 1768, who uses them to reflect on the caprices of fame: he laments that 'Hector's dead name now makes the butcher's dog! / Cato keeps sharp sheep, and Brutus drives a hog!'; elsewhere he mentions Pompey and Caesar as watchdogs, Scipio as a bull-baiter, Nero as a bloodhound, and mourns that Juno, Mars and Venus are often found 'drown'd ... in ditches'.[63] The popularity of these names is amply testified by contemporary sources: Pompey recurs as one of Rev. James Woodforde's greyhounds in 1777, Cato as a 'Pointer Dog' reported lost at Honiton in 1819, Caesar as the hero of Mary Martha

Sherwood's popular children's book of 1818, and Nero, Brutus and Hector as hounds in a disastrous coursing 'excursion' of 1794.[64]

While this selection of names might seem innocuous enough, it gains a darker edge when set against wider cultural trends. In particular, it corresponds closely to the names given to enslaved individuals in the same period. Identical names and types of names appear, for instance, on the headstone of Charles Bacchus, buried at Culworth in 1762, and on the graves of four slaves named Scipio interred at Bristol in 1720, Kirkoswald in 1774, Werrington in 1784 and Nottingham in 1834.[65] Still more are found among Brigadier General Birch's register of Black Loyalists given passage out of New York after the Revolutionary War: among the 3,000 liberated slaves who migrated to Nova Scotia in 1783 are Venus, Dian, Pompey Brown, Sippio Simmons, Ceasor Nicolls, Nero Simmon, Cato Boden and Jenny Bachus, among many others.[66] These conventions were evidently in place by the late seventeenth century: they can already be seen in Aphra Behn's *Oroonoko* (1688), in which the protagonist is renamed Caesar during his captivity in Surinam on the grounds that 'Christians never buy any slaves but they give 'em some name of their own'.[67] Although they took shape in different circumstances, the medieval names Soldan and Turcus can be seen as forerunners of this later habit, based as they are on readiness to equate non-human organisms and non-European peoples.

The central question this raises is why medieval culture should have gravitated towards these specific groups when interpellating animals. Perhaps the best way to resolve this issue is to think of race and class as two sides of a single

coin. At root, both the peasantry and the non-Christian peoples of the Middle East and Mediterranean represent the outermost extremities of medieval culture: one defines the frontiers of Europe very directly, while the other comprises the lowest reach of its social hierarchy. But it is not only in straightforward geographic and economic terms that these groups prove peripheral; they can also be seen as absolute limits of the human, at least in the eyes of the Middle Ages. After all, this is a culture which regarded the edge of the human world not as a hard border, but as a frayed hem that shaded by degrees into bestialism. On the one hand, it accepted as a matter of course that the human form began to unravel into weird hybrid shapes beyond Christendom, populating its travel accounts and *mappae mundi* with lurid images of dog-headed Cynocephali, fish-tailed Sirenes, horned Gegetones, hoofed Hippopedes, and many other such beings.[68] On occasion, animals might even be given primacy over non-European peoples: the conquistador Vasco Núñez de Balboa supposedly awarded his dog Leoniça its own share of slaves after subjugating the Chibchan nations.[69] Perceptions of the peasantry often followed a similar course. Literary sources frequently depict rustics as 'malformed and bestial' creatures, straddling the human and natural orders, as though contaminated by their dedication to agriculture and husbandry.[70] As a consequence, there is a certain logic behind drawing animal names from these groups: they occupy a space that is already liminal, an uncertain hinterland between the human and non-human.

In sum, while names such as Saresyn and Gyll might represent slippage between species and identities, they make obvious that it was not just any point at which the distinction between human and animal might be relaxed. In simple terms, it is only disenfranchised or marginalised groups whose identities are allowed to blur with those of animals; other, more cherished types of identity, whether social, religious or racial at root, are exempted from these ontological cave-ins. As a result, it might be said that the drift between species ends up reinforcing rather than endangering notions of humanness. While it remains true that 'the boundaries of man are much more uncertain and fluctuating' before the Enlightenment, by only making the identities of peasants and non-Christians interchangeable with non-human creatures, medieval culture effectively shored up its own internal hierarchies.[71] Naming might have toyed with the divide between human and animal, but it also honoured the manifold distinctions between human and human. This point then brings us full circle, connecting with one of Derrida's central arguments about the role of language in defining humanity and animality. As he notes in his discussion of Adorno, the same manoeuvres that create the 'vast encampment' of 'living things that man does not recognize as his fellows' can be readily deployed against other human beings, recasting 'hatred of the animal as hatred of the Jew, which one could easily extend, according to the now-familiar outlines of the same logic, to a certain hatred of femininity, even childhood'.[72] Medieval naming sticks closely to this same process, herding together beings without voices and beings deprived of voices.

CHAPTER 6

FINAL CALL: CONCLUSIONS

TOWARDS THE END of Samuel Beckett's 1957 radio-play *All that Fall*, there is a remarkable exchange about language between the central characters Mr and Mrs Rooney. In the middle of Mr Rooney's evasive account of his experiences on board a stalled train, the two suddenly begin to discuss the transience of speech itself. After Mr Rooney reflects that 'sometimes one would think you were struggling with a dead language', and adds that he feels the same about his own words 'when I happen to overhear what I am saying', his wife pronounces: 'well you know, it will be dead in time, just like our own poor dead Gaelic'. These musings are swiftly interrupted, however, by the sound of what Beckett calls an 'urgent baa'. The rude intrusion of an animal voice causes the half-blind Mr Rooney to cry out 'good God!' in alarm; Mrs Rooney's response, however, is more phlegmatic. She muses on how the sheep's noises differ from her own fading voice: 'Oh, the pretty little woolly lamb, crying to suck its mother! Theirs has not changed, since Arcady.' Perhaps predictably, this line of conversation goes no further. After a pause, Mr Rooney returns to his day, asking 'Where was I in my composition?' 'At a standstill', his wife reminds him.[1]

Although this exchange is chiefly concerned with the absurdity of the human condition, and presents the animal as an unwelcome disruption at best, Mrs Rooney's florid words in praise of the 'pretty little woolly lamb' encapsulate a perennial view of the animal world and its difference to that of human beings. By contrasting the 'urgent baa' against her own 'poor dead Gaelic' and its inevitable obsolescence, she sets a rigid line between the timeliness of one and the timelessness of the other. For her, the human world is the world of change and development, growth and decline, where languages and communities form, flourish and 'will be dead in time'; it is the only world in which history is possible, in which past can be recognisably different from present and future. Indeed, Beckett's play wears this history on its sleeve, with its commitment to high modernism and the technologies of railway and radio. Animals on the other hand seem to belong to an order that is immutable, divorced from the transitions that are such a marked part of the human experience, 'not changed, since Arcady'; to echo McHugh, McKay and Miller, Mrs Rooney seems to be asking 'what do beasts know or care of the Renaissance, the Enlightenment, or the avantgarde?'[2] By living in a purely cyclical and instinctual manner, performing behaviours that alter in no perceptible way from generation to generation, animals can have no history equivalent to that of humans, no chronologies or narratives, and no real sense of belonging to any given time period. The voice of the animal is that of eternity itself, a point at which period distinctions can have no meaning: as R. W. Connell states, 'no other species produces and lives in history' aside from humankind.[3]

This is a view that the Middle Ages would recognise, if not wholeheartedly endorse. After all, the period often thought of non-human organisms as timeless statements of their creator, in whose bodies and behaviour eternal truths might be read: as Thomas of Chobham writes in the thirteenth century, 'the Lord created creatures having diverse natures not only for the sustenance of men, but also for their instruction, so through these same creatures not only will we know what is useful in body, but also useful in soul'.[4] Yet while Mrs Rooney's statement might resonate with medieval thinking, it also pricks holes in it. Not merely is Mrs Rooney's sentimentalism ludicrously misplaced, jarring with the play's larger themes of decrepitude, sickness and death, but her reflections fail to add up. One of the passage's chief ironies is that the human characters have arrived 'at a standstill': rather than the animals around them, it is the Rooneys whose lives have fallen into mechanical repetition. Likewise, the fact that Mrs Rooney sees animals speaking from a purely mythic time, being unchanged since the poetic non-place of 'Arcady', underscores that her statement is merely a wistful fantasy. Animals no more belong to an eternal order than the humans that interpret them.

Of course, it does not take a huge leap of imagination to dispel this myth further still, and to reconcile animals with history. In a very direct sense, beasts do have a history, especially those creatures who form part of human society. Even before the agricultural advancements of the eighteenth and nineteenth centuries, and the more recent emergence of the 'zoological, ethological, biological, and genetic forms of knowledge' that exercise Derrida, such organisms as dogs, horses, cats and sheep were products of long processes of

domestication and selective breeding.[5] While medieval ico-
nography might show animals popping into existence as
fully formed species on the fifth day of creation, most of the
creatures encountered on a daily basis in the Middle Ages
were the work of human rather than divine intervention.

But the susceptibility of animals to history also plays
out in other ways too. As this book has hopefully demonstrated, medieval language could not help but register this
history when dealing with animals. The identities it projected on to non-human creatures were never simply neutral, but coloured at the every step by the culture of the
Middle Ages: by its expectations and judgements; by the
concrete uses to which creatures were put; by the emotions
they elicited, and the popular beliefs that framed them; by
the ways in which animals were classified, grouped and
distinguished; by the theoretical centrality of the human
being in relation to other living creatures; and, most trou-
blingly, by the real and notional hierarchies that governed
human beings themselves. Even the culture's parallels with
antiquity say more about its own social structures and
geographic variations, since both determined who might
encounter classical material and what use they might make
of it. In short, naming an animal in the Middle Ages was
never a free choice, but one that took shape in a complex
historical moment.

As a final word, we might wonder how this moment
compares to our own, and the ways in which our language
treats animals in the early twenty-first century. There are
some obvious similarities and equally obvious differences.
On the one hand, many medieval tendencies recognisably look forward to our habits today: currently fashionable

pet-names such as Bella, Teddy, Milo, Lola and Buddy mirror the earlier fondness for diminutive human names that we have seen in Hankyn, Colle, Gibbe and Goby.[6] On the other, we are less likely to give animals unsentimentally functional or overtly racialised names, even if the latter practice persisted well into the twentieth century.[7] But beyond these immediate points of comparison, the names also show a deeper shift in our relationship with other organisms. One conspicuous feature of medieval naming is the breadth of its reference. As we have seen at several points, medieval naming is generous in its expansiveness, and as likely to give names to livestock and wild birds as working and household creatures. Our own culture, however, has seen a radical tightening of interpellation. While we might give our pets elaborate personal names, we do not have our own versions of Watte, Cirgua or Robynet. It is difficult not to see this contraction in light of the industrialisation of food production, and its profound alteration of our experience of the natural world.[8] As Peter Singer notes, modern farming and distribution not only mediate our contact with the animals that we eat and wear but insulate us from them, presenting consumers with 'neat plastic packages' artfully divorced from the 'living, breathing, walking, suffering animal' they contain.[9] Medieval naming, alternatively, does not ignore the interconnectivity between human and animal, with its readiness to see human culture bleeding into the wider landscape, and to attribute human-like personalities to even the remotest creatures. In sum, much like the hierarchy Isidore sketches out, the period's naming systems posit a more truthful sense of the natural world and the place of human beings within it.

NOTES

1. ARE YOU THERE? NAMING AND ITS QUESTIONS

1. See Carolynn van Dyke, 'Naming of the Beasts: Tracking the Animot in Medieval Texts', *Studies in the Age of Chaucer*, 34 (2012), 1–51; Kathleen Walker-Meikle, *Medieval Pets* (Cambridge: Boydell and Brewer, 2012), pp. 16–7; Malcom Jones, *The Secret Middle Ages* (Stroud: Sutton, 2002), pp. 34–61; 'Adrian Room, *The Naming of Animals* (Jefferson, NC: McFarland, 1993)'; Katharina Leibring, 'Animal Names', in Carole Hough (ed.), *Oxford Handbook of Names and Naming* (Oxford: Oxford University Press, 2016), pp. 615–27; Léon Gautier, *La Chevalerie* (Paris: Victor Palmé, 1884), pp. 726–7.

2. See Hazel Harrod, 'A Tale of Two Thieves', in Mody C. Boatright (ed.), *The Sky is My Tipi* (Denton TX: University of North Texas Press, 1949), pp. 207–14.

3. 'Estula', in Willem Noomen and Nico van der Boogaard (eds), *Nouveau recueil complet des fabliaux*, 10 vols (Assen: Van Gorcum, 1983–98), 4:439–42. All translations are my own, unless otherwise stated.

4. J. L. Austin, *How to do Things with Words* (Oxford: Clarendon Press, 1962), pp. 4–11.

5. Bertrand Russell, *An Inquiry into Meaning and Truth* (London: George Allen and Unwin, 1950), p. 63.

6. Roy Harris and Christopher Hutton, *Definition in Theory and Practice: Language, Lexicography and the Law* (London: Continuum, 2007), p. 63.

7. Compare Gaston Duchet-Suchaux, 'Le nom des animaux au Moyen Âge', *Actes des colloques de la Société française d'onomastique*, 12 (2004), 87–90 (p. 89).

8. David Herman, 'Narratology Beyond the Human: Self-Narratives and Inter-Species Identities', in Susan McHugh, Robert McKay and John Miller (eds), *The Palgrave Handbook of Animals and Literature* (London: Palgrave, 2020), p. 61.

9. See Claudia Zatta, *Aristotle and the Animals: The Logos of Life Itself* (Abingdon: Routledge, 2022), pp. 139–42.

2. UNCOMMON NOUNS: HUNTING FOR ANIMAL NAMES

1. See C. A. Mayer, 'La tierce epistre de l'amant verd de Jean Lemaire de Belges', in *De Jean Lemaire de Belges à Jean Giraudoux* (Paris: Nizet, 1970), pp. 27–36; Adrian Armstrong, 'Songe, vision, savoir: l'onirique et l'épistémique chez Molinet et Lemaire de Belges', *Zeitschrift für romanische Philologie*, 123/1 (2007), 50–68; William Calin, 'Jean Lemaire de Belges: courtly narrative at the close of the Middle Ages', in Minnette Grunmann-Gaudel and Robin F. Jones (eds), *The Nature of Medieval Narrative* (Lexington KT: French Forum, 1980), pp. 205–15.

2. See Bernard Ribémont, 'Histoires de perroquets: petit itinéraire zoologique et poétique', *Reinardus*, 8/3 (1990), 155–71; M.T. McMunn, 'Parrots and Poets in Late Medieval Literature', *Anthrozoös*, 12/2 (1999), 68–75.

3. Jean Lemaire de Belges, *Les épîtres de l'amant vert*, ed. Jean Frappier (Geneva: Droz, 1948), pp. 32–7.

4. Suger, *Deeds of Louis the Fat*, trans. Richard C. Cusimano and John Moorhead (Washington DC: Catholic University of America Press, 1992), p. 149; Ranulf Higden, *Polychronicon*, trans. John Trevisa, ed. Charles Babington and J. Rawson Lumby, 9 vols (London: Longman, 1865–86), 8:309; Roger of Wendover, *Flores*

historiarum, ed. Henry Richards Luard, 3 vols (London: Longman, 1890), 1:313.

5. Jacobus de Voragine. *The Golden Legend: Readings on the Saints*, trans. William Granger Ryan, 2 vols (Princeton NJ: Princeton University Press, 2012), 1:532, 177, 228–9.

6. Ugolino Brunforte, *Fioretti di San Francesco*, ed. Antonio Cesari (Palma: Pietro Fiaccadori, 1859), p. 41.

7. Eric Gerald Stanley (ed.), *The Owl and Nightingale* (Manchester: Manchester University Press, 1972), pp. 56, 87.

8. 'In May whan euery herte', in John W. Conlee (ed.), *Middle English Debate Poetry* (East Lansing MI: Colleagues Press, 1991), p. 289.

9. Joyce E. Salisbury, *The Beast Within: Animals in the Middle Ages* (Abingdon: Routledge, 2011), p. 97; Jan M. Ziolkowski, *Talking Animals: Medieval Latin Beast Poetry, 75–1150* (Philadelphia PA: University of Pennsylvania Press, 1993), pp. 241–305.

10. E. P. Evans, *The Criminal Prosecution and Capital Punishment of Animals* (London: William Heinemann, 1906), pp. 335, 358.

11. Lesley Bates MacGregor, 'Criminalising Animals in Medieval France', *Open Library of Humanities*, 5 (2019); Sven Gins, 'Casting Justice Before Swine', *Sophia*, 62 (2023), 631–63 (635).

12. Bruce Thomas Boehrer, Molly Hand and Briar Massumi, 'Animals in the Republic of Letters', in Bruce Thomas Boehrer, Molly Hand and Brian Massumi (eds), *Animals, Animality, and Literature* (Cambridge: Cambridge University Press, 2018), p. 6.

13. Elizabeth Wilson, *Four Centuries of Dog Collars at Leeds Castle* (London: Philip Wilson, 1979), pp. 3–7.

14. Metropolitan Museum of Art, New York, accession number 37.80.1; J. Paul Getty Museum, Los Angeles, MS 7 (85.ML.27), fol. 2v.

15. Anthony Mortimer, *Petrarca's Canzoniere in the English Renaissance* (Amsterdam: Rodopi, 2005), p. 115.

16. Hannah Ryley, *Re-using Manuscripts in Late Medieval England: Repairing, Recycling, Sharing* (Woodbridge: Boydell and Brewer, 2022), pp. 53–4.

17. Ismāʿīl ibn ʿUmar ibn Kathīr, *The Life of the Prophet Muḥammad: A Translation of Al-Sīra Al-Nabawiyya*, trans. Trevor Le Gassick,

4 vols (Reading: Garnet, 1998–2000), 4:513–14. The Qu'ran itself might preserve a dog-name, according to one interpretation of the mysterious term 'Ar-Raqīm' in its version of the Seven Sleepers story (18.9, 18.18); however, the word might equally describe the mountain where the Sleepers' cave was located, or an inscription at its entrance. See Ilse Lichtenstadter, 'Quran and Quran Exegesis', *Humaniora Islamica*, 2 (1974), 3–28 (p.7); W. William Watt, *Companion to the Qur'ān* (London: Allen and Unwin, 1967), p. 139.

18. *The Book of the Discipline* (*Vinaya-piṭaka*): *Cullavagga*, trans. I. B. Horner (London: Pali Text Society, 1952), pp. 272–3; *Grímnismál*, in Ursula Dronke (ed.), *Poetic Edda*, 3 vols (Oxford: Oxford University Press, 1969–2011), 3:119.

19. Saul A. Kripke, *Naming and Necessity* (Cambridge MA: Harvard University Press, 1980), pp. 77–8.

20. Jacques Lacan, *Ecrits*, trans. and ed. Alan Sheridan (London: Tavistock, 1977), p. 148.

21. Corey J. Marvin, *Word Outward: Medieval Perspectives on the Entry into Language* (New York: Routledge, 2001), pp. xvii–xxiii.

22. Cary Wolfe, 'Human, All Too Human: "Animal Studies" and the Humanities', *Publications of the Modern Language Association of America*, 124 (2009), 564–76 (p. 564).

23. Jeremy Bentham, *Chrestomathia*, ed. M. J. Smith and W. H. Burston (Oxford: Clarendon Press, 1983), p. 189.

24. Jacques Derrida, *The Animal That Therefore I Am*, trans. David Wills, ed. Marie-Louise Mallet (New York: Fordham University Press, 2008), p. 32.

25. Cary Wolfe, *Animal Rites: American Culture, the Discourse of Species, and Posthumanist Theory* (Chicago IL: University of Chicago Press, 2003), pp. 41–3; Matthew Senior, 'Classify and Display: Human and Animal Species', in *Animals, Animality, and Literature*, pp. 156–79.

26. Jane Bliss, *Naming and Namelessness in Medieval Romance* (Woodbridge: Boydell, 2008), p. 79.

27. Thomas Duffus Hardy (ed.), *Rotuli litterarum clausarum in Turri*

Londinensi asservati, 2 vols (London: Records Commission, 1833–44), 1:192, 402.

28. Michael Charles Burdet Dawes (ed.), *The Register of Edward the Black Prince*, 4 vols (London: His Majesty's Stationery Office, 1930–3), 4:68–71.

29. William of Pagula, 'The Mirror of King Edward III: Second Version', in Cary J. Nederman (trans. and ed.), *Political Thought in Early-Fourteenth Century England* (Turnhout: Brepols, 2002), p. 117.

30. Léon Ménabréa, 'Notice sur l'ancienne chartreuse de Vallon, en Chablis', *Mémoires de l'académie royale de Savoie*, 2 (1854), 241–307 (p. 294).

31. J. S. Purvis, 'A Note on Sixteenth-Century Farming in Yorkshire', *Yorkshire Archaeological Journal*, 36 (1944), 435–54 (p. 436).

32. James Raine et al. (eds), *Testamenta Eboracensia* 6 vols (London: J. B. Nichols, 1836–1902), 1:69.

33. See Damien Boquet and Piroska Nagy, *Medieval Sensibilities: A History of Emotions in the Middle Ages*, trans. Robert Shaw (Cambridge: Polity Press, 2018); Rita Copeland, *Emotion and the History of Rhetoric in the Middle Ages* (Oxford: Oxford University Press, 2021); Mary C. Flannery, *Emotion and Medieval Textual Media* (Turnhout: Brepols, 2018).

34. Victor Gay and Henri Stein, *Glossaire archaéologique du Moyen Age et de la Renaissance*, 2 vols (Paris: Libraire de la Société Bibliographique, 1887–1928), 1:414. See the discussion in John Block Friedman, 'Dogs in the Identity Formation and Moral Teaching Offered in Some Fifteenth-Century Flemish Manuscript Miniatures', in Laura D. Gelfand (ed.), *Our Dogs, Our Selves: Dogs in Medieval and Early Modern Art, Literature, and Society* (Leiden: Brill, 2016), pp. 325–62 (pp. 355–7).

35. H. E. Chetwynd-Stapylton, *Chronicles of the Yorkshire Family of Stapelton* (London: Bradbury, Agnew and Co., 1884), p. 69; Malcolm Jones, *Secret Middle Ages* (Stroud: Sutton, 2002), p. 35.

36. Elizabeth Porges Watson, 'A Vulpine Martyr: The Fantasy of the Passion of the Fox', *Reinardus*, 6/1 (1993), 105–26.

37. Usama ibn Munqidh, *The Book of Contemplation*, trans. Paul M. Cobb (London: Penguin, 2008), pp. 211–15.

38. Gervais du Bus, *Le roman de Fauvel*, ed. Arthur Langfors (Paris: Firmin Didot, 1919), p. cvii; *Canterbury Interlude*, in John M. Bowers (ed.), *The Canterbury Tales: Fifteenth-Century Continuations and Additions* (Kalamazoo MI: Medieval Institute Publications, 1992), p. 69; John Audelay, 'Marcolf and Solomon', in Susanna Fein (ed.), *Poems and Carols* (Kalamazoo MI: Medieval Institute Publications, 2009), p. 35; John Metham, *Amoryus and Cleopes*, ed. Stephen F. Page (Kalamazoo: Medieval Institute Publications, 1999), p. 38.

39. Nicholas Orme, 'Latin and English Sentences in Fifteenth-Century Schoolbooks', *Yale University Library Gazette*, 60 (1985), 47–57.

40. William Horman, *Vulgaria uiri doctissimi* (London: Richard Pynson, 1519), sig. C1v (STC 13811).

41. John Palsgrave, *L'esclaircissement de la langue francoyse*, ed. F. Génin (Paris: Imprimerie Nationale, 1852), p. 598.

42. Geoffrey Chaucer, *Nun's Priest's Tale*, VII.3383, in *Riverside Chaucer*, gen. ed. Larry D. Benson (Oxford: Oxford University Press, 2008), p. 260.

43. 'Ortus est Canis noster parentibus nobilissimis, patre Megastomo, cuius in familia vestustissima pene innumerabiles clarissimi principes extitere'. Leon Battista Alberti, *Apologhi ed elogi*, ed. Rosario Contarino and Luigi Malerba (Genoa: Edizioni Costa E Nolan, 1984), p. 146.

44. Jeffrey Gantz (trans.), *The Mabinogion* (Harmondsworth: Penguin, 1976), pp.157–60.

45. *Killing of Abel*, in Garrett P. J. Epp (ed.), *The Towneley Plays* (Kalamazoo MI: Medieval Institute Publications, 2017), p. 29.

46. Pieter Beullens, 'Aristotle's Zoology in the Medieval World', in *Animals, Animality, and Literature*, p. 29.

47. Hans Wanner, 'Hundenamen aus dem Anfang des 16. Jahrhunderts', in Karl Friedrich Müller (ed.), *Beiträge zur Sprachwissenschaft und Volkskund* (Lahr: Moritz Schauenburg, 1951), pp. 219–23.

48. *Poetic Edda*, 3:116.

49. Marcelle Thiébaux, *Stag of Love: The Chase in Medieval Literature* (Ithaca NY: Cornell University Press, 1974), p. 185.

50. Elisius Calentius, *La bataille fantastique des roys Rodilardus et Croacus*, ed. P.L. (Geneva: Jean Gay and Sons, 1867).

51. Eugen Kölbing (ed.), *Ipomedon in drei englischen bearbeitungen* (Breslau: W. Koebner, 1889), p. 184.

52. Paul Vincent Spade (trans. and ed.), *Five Texts on the Mediaeval Problem of Universals* (Indianapolis IN: Hackett, 1994), p. 31.

53. Paul Strohm, *Hochon's Arrow: The Social Imagination of Fourteenth-Century Texts* (Princeton NJ: Princeton University Press, 1992), p. 3.

54. 'Ilyf le Messer vulneravit Robertum Pusekat juxta pontem de Corebrigge, ita quod statim obiit': William Page (ed.), *Three Early Assize Rolls for the County of Northumberland* (London: Surtees Society, 1891), p. 76; Jan Jonsjo, *Studies on Middle English Nicknames: Compounds* (Lund: C. W. K. Gleerup, 1979), p. 147.

55. Richard Axton and Peter Happé (eds), *Plays of John Heywood* (Cambridge: Brewer, 1991), p. 90.

56. Peter McLure, 'Interpretation of Hypocoristic Forms of Middle English Baptismal Names', *Nomina*, 21 (1998) 103; William Baldwin, *Beware the Cat*, ed. William A. Ringler and Michael Flachmann (San Marino CA: Huntington Library, 1988), p. 60.

57. William Shakespeare, *Macbeth*, 1.1.8, in William Shakespeare, *Complete Works*, gen. ed. Gary Taylor and Stanley Wells (Oxford: Oxford University Press, 2005), p. 972; Thomas Middleton, *The Witch*, ed. Elizabeth Schafer (London: A. and C. Black, 1994), p. 24; *The Crafty Courtier* (London: John Nutt, 1706), pp. 37–55; Francis Grose, *Classical Dictionary of the Vulgar Tongue* (London: S. Hooper, 1785), p. 108.

58. Helen Parish, '"Paltrie Vermin, Cats, Mise, Toads, and Weasils": Witches, Familiars, and Human-Animal Interactions in the English Witch Trials', in Marina Montesano (ed.), *Witchcraft, Demonology and Magic* (Basel: M. D. P. I., 2020), pp. 84–97 (p. 88). See further Emma Wilby, 'The Witch's Familiar and the Fairy

in Early Modern England and Scotland', *Folklore*, 111/2 (2000), 283–305.

59. Matthew Hopkins, *Discovery of Witches* (London: R. Royston, 1647), p. 2.

60. Richard Bernard, *A Guide to Grand Iury-Men* (London: Felix Kingston, 1627), p. 113 (STC 1943); James A. Serpell, 'Guardian Spirits or Demonic Pets: The Concept of the Witch's Familiar in Early Modern England, 1530–1712', in A. N. H. Creager and W. C. Jordan (eds), *The Human/Animal Boundary* (Cambridge: Cambridge University Press, 1996), pp. 157–90 (p. 175).

61. *Witchcrafts, strange and wonderfull* (London: M. F., 1635), sig. C2 (STC 11107.1); *Gentlemen's Magazine* 29, December 1732, p. 1120.

62. *The most strange and horrible cruelty of Elizabeth Stile* (London: John Allde, 1579), sigs. D2–D3v (STC 11537.5).

63. William Hale and H. T. Ellacombe (eds), *Account of the Executors of Richard Bishop of London* (London: Camden Society, 1874), pp. 58–9. For Hopkins's immediate sources, see Joseph Pentangelo, 'Grizzel Greedigut: A Name "No Mortall Could Invent"', *Names*, 67 (2019), 78–88.

64. Charlotte-Rose Millar, *Witchcraft, the Devil, and Emotions in Early Modern England* (London: Routledge, 2017), p. 36.

3. FORMER ADDRESS: NAMING BEFORE THE MIDDLE AGES

1. Cicero, *De Divinatione*, in William Armistead Falconer et al. (eds), *Cicero*, 29 vols (Cambridge MA: Harvard University Press, 1913–2009), 20:334.

2. Suetonius, *Lives of the Caesars*, in J. C. Rolfe and K. R. Bradley (eds), *Suetonius*, 3 vols (Cambridge MA: Harvard University Press, 1998), 2:150.

3. Crystal Addey, *Divination and Knowledge in Greco-Roman Antiquity* (London: Routledge, 2021); Pauline Ripat, 'Roman Omens, Roman Audiences, and Roman History', *Greece and Rome*, 53 (2006), 155–74. On increased apprehension towards these ideas

during the Middle Ages, see Richard Kieckhefer, *Magic in the Middle Ages* (Cambridge: Cambridge University Press, 2022), pp. 235–60.

4. Juliet Clutton-Brock, *Animals as Domesticates: A World View through History* (East Lansing MI: MSU Press, 2012), pp. 19–34.

5. George A. Reisner, 'Ancient King Gives Dog a Royal Burial', *American Kennel Gazette*, 55 (May, 1938), pp. 7–9 180–2.

6. S. Birch, 'The Tablet of Atefaa II', *Transactions of the Society of Biblical Archaeology*, 4 (1876), 172–94 (pp. 184–5); Richard B. Parkinson (ed.), *Voices from Ancient Egypt* (London: British Museum, 1991), p. 114.

7. G. Maspero, *Guide to the Cairo Museum*, trans. J. E. and A. A. Quibell (Cairo: French Institute of Oriental Archaeology, 1906), pp. 445–66.

8. James Henry Breasted, *Ancient Records of Egypt* III: *The Nineteenth Dynasty* (Chicago IL: University of Chicago Press, 1906), pp. 43, 47, 50, 68, 149, 153, 157.

9. Breasted, *Ancient Records*, p. 201; Herbert Ricke, George R. Hughes and Edward F. Wente, *The Beit el-Wali Temple of Ramesses II* (Chicago IL: The Oriental Institute, 1967), pp. 11, 15.

10. See Salima Ikram, 'Divine Creatures: Animal Mummies', *Divine Creatures: Animal Mummies in Ancient Egypt*, ed. Salima Ikram (Cairo: American University in Cairo Press, 2005), pp. 1–15; Edward Bleiberg, Yekaterina Barbash and Lisa Bruno, *Soulful Creatures: Animal Mummies in Ancient Egypt* (Brooklyn NY: D. Giles, 2013), pp. 19–61.

11. Douglas J. Brewer, Donald B. Redford and Susan Redford, *Domestic Plants and Animals: The Egyptian Origins* (Oxford: Oxbow, 2024), p. 118; George Andrew Reisner, 'The Dog Which Was Honored by the King of Upper and Lower Egypt', *Bulletin of the Museum of Fine Arts*, 34 (1936), 96–9 (p. 99).

12. Jaromir Málek, *The Cat in Ancient Egypt* (London: British Museum Press, 1993) pp. 124–5; Norman de Garis Davies, *The Tomb of Puyemrê at Thebes* I: *The Hall of Memories* (New York: Metropolitan Museum of Art, 1922), pp. 36–7.

C

13. See Daniela Rosenow, 'The Naos of Bastet, Lady of the Shrine from Bubastis', *Journal of Egyptian Archaeology*, 94 (2008), 247–66.

14. Homer, *Odyssey*, 17.290–326, 2 vols, trans. and ed. A. T. Murray and George Dimock (Cambridge MA: Harvard University Press, 2004), 2:176.

15. Virgil, *Aeneid*, 11.89–90, in H. Rushton Fairclough and G. P. Goold (eds), *Virgil*, 2 vols (Cambridge MA: Harvard University Press, 2000), 2:242.

16. J. M. C. Toynbee, 'Beasts and their Names in the Roman Empire', *Papers of the British School at Rome*, 16 (1948), pp. 24–37 (p. 36); Procopius, *History of the Wars*, trans. and ed. H. R. Dewing, 5 vols (Cambridge MA: Harvard University Press, 1935), 4:400–3. On the possible meanings of Porphyrios's name, see Anthony Kaldellis, *A Cabinet of Byzantine Curiosities* (Oxford: Oxford University Press, 2017), p. 32.

17. Plutarch, *Isis and Osiris*, in Frank Cole Babbitt (trans. and ed.), *Moralia*, 15 vols (Cambridge MA: Harvard University Press, 1936), 5:28–9.

18. Aristophanes, *Fragments*, trans. and ed. Jeffrey Henderson (Cambridge MA: Harvard University Press, 2008), p. 138.

19. *Battle of Frogs and Mice*, in Martin L. West (trans. and ed.), *Homeric Hymns. Homeric Apocrypha. Lives of Homer* (Cambridge MA: Harvard University Press, 2003), pp. 265–93; *Testamentum Porcelli*, in F. Buecheler (ed.), *Petronii Satirae et Liber Priapeorum* (Berlin: Weidmann 1882), pp. 241–2.

20. While the archaeological record shows the importance of pork in the Roman diet, especially in urban areas, it is doubtful that pigs would carry names: see Edward Champlin, 'The Testament of the Piglet', *Phoenix*, 41 (1987), 174–83. There are very few references to named pigs in antiquity; a typically ambiguous example is Plutarch's Gryllus (Grunter) from the dialogue 'Bruta animalia ratione uti', although Gryllus is supposedly a sailor transformed by Circe. See Babbitt (trans. and ed.), *Moralia*, 12:492–533.

21. Homer, *Iliad*, 8.186, 19.406, 23.295, trans. and ed. A. T. Murray

and William F. Wyatt, 2 vols (Cambridge MA: Harvard University Press, 1999), 1:364–5, 2:364–5, 2:514–5.

22. Ovid, *Metamorphoses*, 3.206–34, ed. Frank Justus Miller and G. P. Goold, 2 vols (Cambridge MA: Harvard University Press, 1977), 1:138–41.

23. Hyginus, *Fabulae*, ed. P. K. Marshall (Stuttgart: B. G. Teubner Verlagsgesellschaft, 1993), pp. 150–1; Virgil, *Eclogues*, 8.107, in Fairclough and Goold (eds), *Virgil*, 1:82; Columella, *On Agriculture*, ed. E. S. Forster and Edward H. Heffner, 3 vols (Cambridge MA: Harvard University Press, 1968), 2:314; Julius Pollux, *Onomasticon*, ed. Immanuel Bekker (Berlin: Libraria Friderici Nicolai, 1846), p. 202.

24. *Eclogues* 3.17–8, 1:38; Julius Pollux, *Onomasticon*, p. 202.

25. Xenophon, *On Hunting*, in E. C. Marchant and G. W. Bowersock (trans. and eds), *Scripta minora* (Cambridge MA: Harvard University Press, 1968), p. 414; Arrian, *Kynegetikos*, in A. G. Roos and Gerhard Wirth (eds), *Flavius Arrianus: Scripta minora et fragmenta* (Munich and Leipzig: K. G. Saur Verlag, 2002), p. 82; Rudolf Wachter, 'Inscriptions on the François Vase', *Museum Helveticum*, 48 (1991), 87–8.

26. Homer, *Iliad*, 8.186, 1:364–5.

27. Maria Grazia Granino Cecere, 'Il sepolcro de la catella Aeolis', *Zeitschrift für Papyrologie und Epigraphik*, 100 (1994), 413–21 (p. 414).

28. Suetonius, *Lives*, 1:498; David Magie and David Rohrbacher (eds), *Historia Augusta*, 3 vols (Cambridge MA: Harvard University Press, 2022), 1:218.

29. Theocritus, *Idylls*, 8.65, in Neil Hopkinson (trans. and ed.), *Theocritus. Moschus. Bion* (Cambridge MA: Harvard University Press, 2015), pp. 144–5.

30. W. R. Paton (ed.), *Greek Anthology*, 7.212, 5 vols (Cambridge MA: Harvard University Press, 1914–8), 2:120.

31. J. M. C. Toynbee, *Animals in Roman Life and Art* (Ithaca NY: Cornell University Press, 1973), p. 134.

32. Pliny the Elder, *Natural History*, ed. H. Rackham, W. H. S. Jones

C

and D. E. Eichholz, 10 vols (Cambridge MA: Harvard University Press, 1938–62), 3:10.

33. John Chadwick, J. T. Killen and J.-P. Oliver, *The Knossos Tablets* (Cambridge: Cambridge University Press, 1971), pp. 46–7; J. T. Killen, 'The Oxen's names on the Knossos Ch tablets', *Minos*, 27–8 (1992–3), 101–7; Mika Kajava, 'Jpa-ko-qe (KN Ch 5728): A New Ox Name from Knossos?', *Arctos*, 45 (2011), 59–70 (pp. 60–1).

34. Theodor Mommsen et al., *Corpus Inscriptionum Latinarum*, 17 vols (Berlin: Georgius Reimerus; Deutsche Akademie der Wissenschaften zu Berlin, 1871–2015), 6:2903, 13:63 (numbers 29896 and 488). The accession number for the Margarita tablet is 1756,0101.1126.

35. See Constance Classen, *The Deepest Sense: A Cultural History of Touch* (Urbana IL: University of Illinois Press, 2012), p. 99.

36. Theocritus, *Idylls*, 4.45, p. 76; Kajava, 'Jpa-ko-qe', p. 59.

37. Toynbee, *Animals in Roman Life*, pp. 95–6; Dimas Fernández-Galiano, *Carranque, centro di Hispania romano* (Alcalá: Museo Arqueológico Regional, 2001); Michael Kulikowski, *Late Roman Spain and Its Cities* (Baltimore MD: Johns Hopkins University Press, 2005), pp. 145–7.

38. Dio Chrysostom, *Discourses*, ed. H. Lamar Crosby, 5 vols (Cambridge MA: Harvard University Press, 1932–51), 4:36. Podargos is the usual transliteration of Linear B Po-da-ko: see Killen, 'Oxen's names'.

39. Xenophon, *On Hunting*, p. 414; Homer, *Iliad*, 16.149, pp. 172–3; Pseudo-Apollodorus, *The Library*, 3.4.4, trans. and ed. James G. Frazer, 2 vols (Cambridge MA: Harvard University Press, 1921), 1:324; Theocritus, *Idylls*, 4.45, p. 76. Rumpel reads Lépargos as the name of a cowherd's dog in his *Lexicon Theocriteum* (Leipzig: B. G. Teubner, 1889), p. 164.

40. Jacques Derrida, *The Animal That Therefore I Am*, trans. David Wills (New York: Fordham University Press, 2008), p. 48.

41. Plutarch, *Alexander*, in Bernadotte Perrin (trans. and ed.), *Lives*, 11 vols (Cambridge MA: Harvard University Press, 1914–26), 7:398; Philostratus of Athens, *Life of Apollonius of Tyana*, trans.

and ed. Christopher P. Jones, 3 vols (Cambridge MA: Harvard University Press, 2005–6), 1:158.

42. Joannes Xiphilinus, *Epitome Dionis*, in Cassius Dio, *Romaikon historion*, ed. Freidrich Wilhelm Sturz, 4 vols (Leipzig: Libraria Kuehniana, 1824–7), 4:368–9.

43. Suetonius, *Lives*, 1:498.

44. Dio Cassius, *Roman History*, trans. and ed. Earnest Cary and Herbert B. Foster (Cambridge MA: Harvard University Press, 1914–27), 9:352; Ammianus Marcellinus, *History*, ed. J. C. Rolfe, 3 vols (Cambridge MA: Harvard University Press, 1939–50), 3:238.

45. *Historia Augusta*, 1:206–7; Procopius, *History of the Wars*, 3.2.25–26, 2:16.

46. Al-Balādhurī, *Ansāb Al-ashrāf*, ed. Max Schloessinger, M. J. Kister and S. D. F. Goitein, 5 vols (Jerusalem: Hebrew University Press, 1936–71), 4.B.1.16; Abūal-'Alā' al-Ma'arrī, *Epistle of Forgiveness*, trans. and ed. G. J. H. van Gelder and Gregor Schoeler (New York: New York University Press, 2013–4), 2:75.

47. Procopius, *History of the Wars*, 2:16.

48. Ibn Wādiḥ Al Ya'qūbī, *Ta'rikh*, *Works*, trans. and ed. Matthew S. Gordon et al., 3 vols (Leiden: Brill, 2018), 3:891, 904; Tahera Qutbuddin, 'The Evolution of Early Arabic Oration', in Beatrice Gruendler and Michael Cooperson (eds), *Classical Arabic Humanities in Their Own Terms* (Leiden: Brill, 2008), pp. 176–273 (p. 262).

49. *Historia Augusta*, 1:218–9.

50. See, for instance, Ernst Robert Curtius, *European Literature and the Latin Middle Ages*, trans. Willard Trask (Princeton NJ: Princeton University Press, 1953), pp. 36–61; Robert Black, *Humanism and Education in Medieval and Renaissance Italy* (Cambridge: Cambridge University Press, 2004), pp. 64–172.

51. Hesiod, *Theogony*, 309, in Glenn W. Most (trans. and ed.), *Hesiod*, 2 vols (Cambridge MA: Harvard University Press, 2018), 1:26; Theocritus, *Idylls*, 25.139, p. 352.

52. Plutarch, *Theseus*, in Perrin (trans. and ed.), *Lives*, 1:18–21.

53. Callimachus, 'Hymn to Zeus', 49, in Dee L. Clayman (trans. and

ed.), *Hecale. Hymns. Epigrams* (Cambridge MA: Harvard University Press, 2022), pp. 186–7.

54. Pseudo-Apollodorus, *The Library*, 3.14.7, 2:96.

55. Wachter, 'Inscriptions', pp. 87–8.

56. Jamie Kreiner, *Legions of Pigs in the Medieval West* (New Haven CT: Yale, 2020), p. 22.

57. Carl C. Schlam, 'Diana and Actaeon: Metamorphoses of a Myth', *Classical Antiquity*, 3/1 (1984), 82–110.

58. Pliny, *Natural History*, 3:100–1.

59. Hermann Oesterley (ed.), *Gesta Romanorum*, 2 vols (Berlin: Weidmannsche Buchhandlung, 1872), 2:496–8; Carl Rikard Unger (ed.), *Saga Điðriks konungs af Bern* (Copenhagen: Feilberg and Landmarks Forlag, 1853), p. 235.

60. Julius Pollux, *Onomasticon*, p. 202.

61. *Greek Anthology*, 7.212, 7.211, 7.199, 2:118–21, 112–13.

62. Cecere, 'Il sepolcro della catella', p. 419; Giovanni Lettich (ed.), *Iscrizioni romane di Iulia Concordia* (Trieste: Centro studi storico-religiosi Friuli-Venezia Giulia, 1994), 1:3:276; Mommsen et al., *Corpus Inscriptionum Latinarum*, 6:4:1:2903, 6:4:3:4043, 10:1:74 (numbers 29895, 39093, 659).

63. Cecere, 'Il sepolcro della catella', p. 419; Mommsen et al., *Corpus Inscriptionum Latinarum*, 6:3:2062 (number 19190).

64. Martial, *Epigrams*, 1.109, 11.69, ed. D.R. Shackleton Bailey, 3 vols (Cambridge MA: Harvard University Press, 1993), 1:120, 3:58–60.

65. Dio Chrysostom, *Discourses*, 4:36.

66. C.V. Rangaswami, 'Memorials for Pets, Animals and Heroes', *Memorial Stones: A Study of Their Origin, Significance, and Variety*, ed. S. Settar and Günther-Dietz Sontheimer (Dharwar: Institute of Indian Art History, 1982), p. 240; K. A. Nilakantra Sastri, *History of South India from Prehistoric Times to the Fall of Vijayanagar* (Oxford: Oxford University Press, 1975), p. 326.

67. 'Le blonc et le beau chien courant': Jacques de Brézé, *La Chasse, les Dits du bon chien Souillard et les Louanges de Madame Anne de France*, ed. Gunnar Tilander (Lund: Bloms, 1959), p. 56.

68. 'Care Zabot, tibi parva domus, breve corpus habebas / Et tumulus brevis est, et breve carmen habe': Marco Vattasso (ed.), I *codici Petrarcheschi della Biblioteca Vaticana* (Rome: Tipografia poliglotta Vaticana, 1908), p. 5.

69. See, for instance, Daniela Pizzagalli, *La signora del Rinascimento: Vita e splendori di Isabella d'Este alla corte di Mantova* (Milan: Rizzoli, 2001); George R. Marek, *The Bed and the Throne: The Life of Isabella d'Este* (New York: Harper and Row, 1976).

70. 'Pouero Martino di bona memoria con vniuersal dolore della corte': Kathleen Walker-Meikle, *Medieval Pets* (Woodbridge: Boydell, 2012), p. 127, n. 57.

71. Alessandro Luzio and Rodolfo Renier, *La coltura e le relazioni letterarie di Isabella d'Este Gonzaga* (Milan: Sylvestre Bonnard, 2006), pp. 30–1. Walker-Meikle appends the sequence of dedicatory verse for Aura to her 'Late Medieval Pet-Keeping' (unpublished PhD thesis, University College London, 2013), pp. 206–49.

72. Ulisse Aldrovandi, *De quadripedibus digitatis viviparis, libri tres* (Bologna: Niccolo Tobaldini, 1637), pp. 524–5.

73. 'Orinae catellae, coelesti caniculae forma fide iocis': Giovanni Battista, 'Il Monasterio di Santa Orsola in Mantova', *Archivio storico Lombardo*, 4 (1895), 167–86 (p .178).

74. Alexander Reise (ed.), *Anthologica Latina*, 3 vols (Leipzig: B. G. Tuebner, 1868–1926), 1:1.211; Toynbee, *Animals in Roman Life*, pp. 96–7.

75. William Langland, *Piers Plowman: The B-text*, 19 269–74, ed. A. V. C. Schmidt (London: Dent, 1978), p. 244.

76. Jean-Claude Schmitt, *Le saint lévrier: Guinefort, guérisseur d'enfants depuis le XIIIe siècle* (Paris: Flammarion, 1979).

77. Étienne de Bourbon, *Anecdotes historiques légendes et apologues* (Paris: Libraire Renouard, 1877), pp. 325–8.

78. Katherine M. D. Dunbabin, *Mosaics of the Greek and Roman World* (Cambridge: Cambridge University Press, 1999), pp. 97–100.

79. Toynbee, *Animals in Roman Life*, pp. 95–8; Sîan Lewis and Lloyd Llewellyn-Jones, *The Culture of Animals in Antiquity* (London: Routledge, 2018), pp. 704–5.

80. James Dean (ed.), *Richard the Redeless and Mum and the Sothsegger* (Kalamazoo MI: Medieval Institute Publications, 2000), p. 38; 'Hic tibi qua portus Belini est, sculptilis ursa ... nuncupat hanc vulgus Bossam cognomine': William Lily, *Antibossicon* (London: Richard Pynson, 1521), fol. 2 (STC 15606).

81. Martha Carlin, *Medieval Southwark* (London: Hambledon Press, 1996), pp. 60–1; John Taylor, *Bull, Beare, and Horse* (London: M. Parsons, 1638), sigs. D8–D8v (STC 23739).

4.   TYPE CASTING: NAMING AND SPECIES

1.   See Georges Cuvier, *The Animal Kingdom*, trans. Edward Griffith, 16 vols (London: George Whittaker, 1827–35), 1:18–21, 39–48; Paul Lawrence Farber, *Finding Order in Nature: The Naturalist Tradition* (Baltimore MD: Johns Hopkins, 2003), pp. 6–21, 37–45.

2.   Charles Darwin, *On the Origin of Species by Means of Natural Selection* (London: John Murray, 1859), pp. 467–8.

3.   N. Gontier, 'Depicting the Tree of Life: The Philosophical and Historical Roots of Evolutionary Tree Diagrams', *Evolution, Education, Outreach*, 4 (2011), 515–38; Gowan Dawson, *Monkey to Man: The Evolution of the March of Progress Image* (New Haven CT: Yale University Press, 2024), p. 118.

4.   John S. Wilkins, *Species: A History of the Idea* (Berkeley CA: University of California Press, 2009), pp. 35–46; Susan Crane, *Animal Encounters: Contacts and Concepts in Medieval Britain* (Pittsburgh PA: University of Pennslyvania Press, 2012), pp. 69–100.

5.   Arthur O. Lovejoy, *The Great Chain of Being: A Study of the History of an Idea* (Cambridge MA: Harvard University Press, 1936), pp. 67–98.

6.   On Isidore's later influence, see Richard Barber, *Bestiary: Being an English Version of the Bodleian Library, Oxford MS Bodley 764* (Woodbridge: Boydell, 1993), pp. 71, 102.

7.   'Nihil autem sagacius canibus; plus enim sensus ceteris animalibus habent. Namque soli sua nomina recognoscunt; dominos suos diligunt; dominorum tecta defendunt': Isidorus

Hispalensis, *Etymologiae sive originum*, 12.2.25–6, ed. W. M Lindsay, 2 vols (Oxford: Clarendon Press, 1911), n.p.

8.   'Vivacitas equorum multa: exultant enim in campis; odorantur bellum; excitantur sono tubae ad proelium; voce accensi ad cursum provocantur; dolent cum victi fuerint; exultant cum vicerint ... interfectis vel morientibus dominis multi lacrimas fundunt. Solum enim equum propter hominem lacrimare et doloris affectum sentire': Isidore, *Etymologiae*, 12.1.43.

9.   'In Centauris equorum et hominum natura permixta est': Isidore, *Etymologiae*, 12.1.43.

10.   Jorge Luis Borges, 'The Analytical Language of John Wilkins', in *Other Inquisitions*, 1937–1952, trans. R. L. C. Simms (London: Souvenir Press, 1973), pp. 101–5; Michel Foucault, *The Order of Things* (London: Routledge, 1970), p. xvi.

11.   Cary Wolfe, *Animal Rites: American Culture, the Discourse of Species, and Posthumanist Theory* (Chicago IL: University of Chicago Press, 2003), p. 192.

12.   Hans Wanner, 'Hundenamen aus dem Anfang des 16. Jahrhunderts', in Karl Friedrich Müller (ed.), *Beiträge zur Sprachwissenschaft und Volkskunde* (Lahr: Moritz Schauenburg, 1951), pp. 219–23.

13.   David Scott-Macnab, 'The Names of All Manner of Hounds: A Unique Inventory in a Fifteenth-Century Manuscript', *Viator*, 44 (2013), 339–68. Despite its uniqueness and value, the current whereabouts of the manuscript are unknown; it was sold to an anonymous buyer at Christie's in January 2006. See *Rare Book Review*, 33/1 (February/March 2006), 20.

14.   Corinne Beck and Fabrice Guizard, 'Être chien, être cheval au Moyen Âge: Quelles sources pour atteindre la condition des animaux?', in Éric Baratay (ed.), *Aux sources de l'histoire animale* (Paris: Éditions de la Sorbonne, 2019), pp. 129–38 (p. 132).

15.   On the development of this idea after the Middle Ages, see Michael Worboys, Julie-Marie Strange and Neil Pemberton, *The Invention of the Modern Dog: Breed and Blood in Victorian Britain* (Baltimore MD: Johns Hopkins University Press, 2018), pp. 23–53.

16. John Gower, *Visio Anglie*, 394–414, in G. C. Macauley (ed.), *Complete Works: The Latin Works* (Oxford: Oxford University Press, 1902), p. 33.

17. Michaele Angelus Blondus, *De Canibus et venatione* (Rome: Antonius Bladus Asulanus, 1544), fols 4v–6v.

18. W. Hastings Kelke, 'On Three Sepulchral Monuments at Clifton Reynes in the County of Buckingham', *Archaeological Journal*, 11 (1854), 149–56 (p. 154); David Lyndsay, *Complaynt and Publict Confessioun of the Kingis Auld Hound*, in David Laing (ed.), *Poetical Works* (Edinburgh: William Patterson, 1871), 1:111.

19. National Portrait Gallery D33230; H. E. Chetwynd-Stapylton, *Chronicles of the Yorkshire Family of Stapelton* (London: Bradbury, Agnew and Co., 1884), p. 69; Norman Davis, Richard Beadle and Colin Richmond (eds), *Paston Letters and Papers of the Fifteenth Century*, 3 vols (Oxford: Clarendon Press, 2004–5), 1:476.

20. Gottfried von Strassburg, *Tristan und Isolde*, ed. Dieter Kühn (Frankfurt: S. Fischer, 2003), p. 761.

21. This interpretation seems to originate with Marie Louise Bruce, *Anne Boleyn: A Biography* (New York: Coward, McCann and Geoghegan, 1972), p. 243.

22. State Papers Foreign and Domestic, Henry VIII Lisle Papers, SP 310, f. 70. The source of the error seems to be James Gairdner (ed.), *Letters and Papers, Foreign and Domestic, of the Reign of Henry VIII* (London: HM Stationery Office, 1886), 9:335. 'Purkoy' appears in multiple fictionalisations of Anne's downfall, beginning with Edith Sitwell's *Fanfare for Elizabeth* (New York: MacMillan, 1946), pp. 67–8, and continuing through the novels of Hilary Mantel, Philippa Gregory, Alison Weir and others.

23. Sei Shōnagon, *Pillow Book*, trans. and ed. Ivan Morris (Harmondsworth: Penguin, 1967), pp. 30–3; Ivan Morris, 'Okinamaro', *The Journal-Newsletter of the Association of Teachers of Japanese*, 2 (1964), 1–5 (p. 3).

24. Achille Harlay de Sancy, 'Confession Catholique', in *Recueil de Diverses Pièces, Servant à l'Histoire de Henry III* (Cologne: Pierre du Marteau, 1666), pp. 348–9.

25. Ernst Götzinger, *Reallexikon der deutschen Altertümer* (Leipzig: Woldemar Urban, 1881), p. 508.

26. Francisco Lopez de Gómara, *La seconda parte delle Historie generali dell'India* (Venice: Giordano Ziletti, 1557), fol. 55v.

27. Friedrich W. D. Brie (ed.), *The Brut, or The Chronicles of England*, 2 vols (London: Kegan Paul, Trench, Trübner and Co., 1906–8), 2:581; Bodleian Library, Oxford, MS Rawlinson D.939, section 1r.

28. *Paston Letters and Papers*, 1:603.

29. Michael Drayton, *Moon-Calfe*, 1127–8, in *Works*, 5 vols (Oxford: Oxford University Press, 1961), 3:195.

30. 'Oyez, a Bemonde, done, oyez, huy, a luy est, dount a luy est, auaunt, a Bemond, auant, ho syre': William Twiti, *The Art of Hunting*, ed. Bror Danielsson (Stokholm: Almcvist och Wiksell, 1977), p. 55.

31. Carl Rikard Unger (ed.), *Saga Điðriks konungs af Bern* (Copenhagen: Feilberg and Landmarks Forlag, 1853), p. 235; Jón Böðvarsson (ed.), *Brennu-Njáls saga*, 2 vols (Reykjavik: Prentsmiðja Jóns Helgasonar, 1970), 1:171.

32. Ovid, *Metamorphoses*, trans. Arthur Golding, ed. John Frederick Nims (Philadelphia PA: Paul Dry, 2000), pp. 68–9; Ovid, *Metamorphosis Englished*, trans. George Sandys (London: William Stansby, 1626), pp. 50–1 (STC 18964); Abraham Fraunce, *The Third Part of the Countesse of Pembrokes Yuychurch*, ed. Gerald Snare (Berkeley CA: California State University Press, 1975), p. 111.

33. Nennius, *Historia Britonum*, ed. Joseph Stevenson (London: English Historical Society, 1838), p. 60; *Guth gadair i cCnoc na Rig*, in Ruth P.M. Lehmann (ed.), *Early Irish Verse* (Austin TX: University of Texas Press, 1982), p. 80; Blondus, *De Canibus*, fol. 4v.

34. Gonzalo Fernández de Oviedo, *Historia general y natural de las Indias*, ed. José Amador de los Ríos, 4 vols (Madrid: Real Academia de la Historia, 1851–3), 2:3.

35. Blondus, *De Canibus*, fol. 4v; Ovid, *Metamorphoses*, trans. Golding, p. 68; Ovid, *Metamorphosis*, trans. Sandys, pp. 50–1; Scott-Macnab, 'Names', pp. 363, 357–8.

36. Fraunce, *Third Part*, p. 111; George Chapman, *Gentleman Usher*, ed. John Hazel Smith (Lincoln: University of Nebraska Press, 1970), p. 11; William Shakespeare, *Merry Wives of Windsor*, 2.1.100–8, in *Complete Works*, gen. ed. Gary Taylor and Stanley Wells (Oxford: Oxford University Press, 2005), p. 518; Richard Robinson, A *Golden Mirrour* (London: Roger Ward, 1589), sig. C3 (STC 21121.5); John Harington, *Metamorphosis of Ajax*, ed. Elizabeth Story Donno (New York: Columbia University Press, 1962), p. 110; Tobias Hume, 'Hunting Song', in Edward Doughtie (ed.), *Lyrics from English Airs, 1596–1622* (New Haven CT: Harvard University Press, 1970), p. 288; Izaak Walton, *The Complete Angler*, ed. Andrew Lang (London: Dent, 1958), p. 47.

37. 'Kladdwyd kilhart kelfydd ymlyniad/ ymlaenav Evionydd … parer dydd y heliai hydd': Patrick Sims-Williams (ed.), *The Medieval Welsh Englynion Y Beddau* (Woodbridge: Boydell and Brewer, 2023), p. 24.

38. Béroul, *Le Roman de Tristan* (Paris: Librairie H. Champion, 1970), pp. 80–4; Lyndsay, *Complaynt and Publict Confesioun*, 1:111; Hermann Oesterley (ed.), *Gesta Romanorum* (Berlin: Weidmann, 1872), 2:496–8; Scott-Macnab, 'Names', pp. 361, 365. The translations of the *Gesta* names are provided by the text itself: 'Richer et Emulemyn currunt ad cervos et ursos … Hanegif id est accipite et donate'.

39. See further Bohdana Librova, 'Quelques observations sur les emplois figurés des noms du chien en français médiéval', in Dora Faraci (ed.), *Simbolismo animale e letteratura* (Manziana: Vecchiarelli, 2003), pp. 61–88.

40. Valéria Tóth, *Personal Names in a Medieval Context* (Hamburg: Buske, 2022), p. 129; Friedrich von Hagedorn, *Moralische Gedichte* (Hamburg: Johann Carl Bohn, 1753), p. 160; Karl Rygh, N*orske og islandiske tilnavne fra oldtiden og middelalderen* (s.l.: s.n., 1800), p. 61. Rover is first documented in the third edition of Nicholas Cox's *Gentlemans Recreation*, 4 vols (London: Freeman Collins, 1686), 1:19 (Wing C6704); an early Fido (Faithful) is Viscount Cobham's Italian greyhound, memorialised on the 'Temple of British

Worthies' at Stowe House in 1735, alongside Newton, Milton and Bacon.

41. W. Carew Hazlitt (ed.), *Shakespeare Jest-books* (London: Willis and Sotheran, 1864), pp. 98–9.

42. Robert Fabyan, *New Chronicles of England and France*, ed. Henry Ellis (London: F. C. and J. Rivington et al., 1811), p. 672.

43. *Historie of Iacob and Esau* (London: Henry Bynneman, 1568), sig. A2 (STC 14327).

44. V. J. Scattergood, *Politics and Poetry in the Fifteenth Century, 1399–1485* (London: Blandford, 1971), p. 178.

45. Frederick J. Furnivall, *Hymns to the Virgin and Christ and other Religious Pieces* (London: Kegan Paul, Trench, Trübner and Co., 1857), p. 61.

46. Jacobo Sannazaro, *Arcadia*, ed. Alfredo Mauri (Turin: Einaudi, 2000), p. 108.

47. J. R. R. Tolkien, E. V. Gordon and Norman Davs (eds), *Sir Gawain and the Green Knight* (Oxford: Oxford University Press, 1967), pp. 21–2; Paul Meyer (ed.), *L'Histoire de Guillaume le Maréchal*, 3 vols (Paris: Librairie Renouard, 1891), 1:49; Colin Smith (ed.), *Poema de mio Cid* (Oxford: Clarendon Press, 1972), pp. 50–1; *Thomas Malory, Le Morte Darthur*, ed. Stephen H.A. Shepherd (New York: Norton, 2004), p. 15.

48. Joseph J. Duggan and Karen Akiyama (ed.), *La Chanson de Roland*, 3342, 1153, 1491, 1531, 1554, 2 vols (Turnhout: Brepols, 2005), 1:243, 157, 170–2.

49. Ferdinand Castets (ed.), *Quatre Fils Aymon*, 55C9, 8260 (Geneva: Slatkine, 1974), pp. 435, 525; Mario Eusebi (ed.), *Chevalerie Ogier de Danemarche*, 3446 (Milan: Istituto editoriale cisalpino, 1963), p. 178.

50. *Grímnismál*, in Ursula Dronke (ed.), *Poetic Edda*, 3 vols (Oxford: Oxford University Press, 1969–2011), 3:119.

51. T. W. Machen (ed.), *Vafþrúðnismál*, 12.1, 14.1 (Turnhout: Brepols, 2008), pp. 60–1; Snorri Sturluson, *Edda*, ed. Finnur Jónsson (Copenhagen: G. E. C. Gad, 1900), pp. 42–3.

52. Melissa Furrow, 'A Minor Comic Poem in a Major Romance Manuscript: "Lyarde"', *Forum for Modern Language Studies*, 32

(1996), 289–302; 'Ty the mare, tom boy', in Joseph Ritson (ed.), *Ancient Songs* (London: J. Johnson, 1790), pp. 130–3; Geoffrey Chaucer, *Troilus and Criseyde*, I.218–25 and *Canterbury Tales*, I.4115, I.616, in *Riverside Chaucer*, gen. ed. Larry D. Benson (Oxford: Oxford University Press, 2008), pp. 476, 81, 33.

53. Reginald R. Sharpe (ed.), *Calendar of Wills Proved and Enrolled in the Court of Hustings*, 2 vols (London: John C. Francis, 1889–90), 1:689, 2:85; Mihailo Dinić, 'Dubrovačka srednjevekovna karavanska trgovina', *Jugoslovenski istorijski časopis*, 3 (1937), 119–46 (p. 135); J. Y. W. Lloyd, *The History of The Princes, The Lords Marcher, and the Ancient Nobility of Powys Fadog*, 6 vols (London: Whiting and Co., 1881–7), 1:380; David Blair Foss, 'The Canterbury Archiepiscopates of John Stafford (1443–52) and John Kemp (1452–54)', 3 vols (unpublished PhD thesis, King's College London, 1986), 3:130.

54. A. Z. Helcel et al. (eds), *Starodawne prawa polskiego pomniki*, 12 vols (Warsaw: Gustawa Sennewalda, Akademia Umiejętności, 1856–1921), 1:256; Chaucer, *Friar's Tale*, III.1544, in *Riverside Chaucer*, p. 126.

55. Peter Northeast and Heather Falvey (eds), *Wills of the Archdeaconry of Sudbury 1439–1474*, 2 vols (Woodbridge: Boydell, 2001–10), 1:410; R. B. Cook, 'Wills of Leeds and District', *Thoresby Society Publications*, 22 (1915), 85–103, 235–66 (p. 259); James Raine et al. (eds), *Testamenta Eboracensis*, 6 vols (London: J. B. Nichols, 1836–1902), 1:341.

56. *Quatre Fils Aymon*, 1815–17, p. 214, et passim.

57. Carly Ameen et al., 'In search of the "great horse": a zooarchaeological assessment of horses from England (AD 300–1650)', *International Journal of Osteoarchaeology*, 31 (2021), 1247–57.

58. John Fisher, 'Chaucer's Horses', *South Atlantic Quarterly*, 60 (1961), 71–9; Rodney Delasanta, 'The Horsemen of the "Canterbury Tales"', *Chaucer Review*, 3 (1968), 29–36; Beryl Rowland, 'The Horse and Rider Figure in Chaucer's Works', *University of Toronto Quarterly*, 35 (1966), 246–59.

59. Heather Dail, 'Silent Translators: The Role of the Animal as a Mediator in Medieval Human Relationships', in Krishanu Maiti and Soumyadeep Chakraborty (eds), *Global Perspectives on Eco-Aesthetics and Eco-Ethics: A Green Critique* (Lanham MD: Rowman and Littlefield, 2020), pp. 255–64 (p. 257).

60. William Hale (ed.), *Account of the Executors of Richard Bishop of London* (London: Camden Society, 1874), pp. 58–9; Georges Musset, 'Chartrier de Pons II', *Archives Historiques de la Saintonge et de l'Aunis*, 21 (1892), 1–427 (p. 169); Frederick J. Furnivall, (ed.), *Fifty Earliest English Wills* (Oxford: Oxford University Press, 1964), p. 53.

61. Luigi Cibrario, *Memorie Storiche* (Turin: Eredi Botta, 1868), pp. 50–1.

62. *Calendar of Close Rolls, Edward III: 1339–1341* (London: Her Majesty's Stationery Office, 1901), p. 547.

63. *Testamenta Eboracensia*, 1:186; *Calendar of Wills Proved and Enrolled*, 2:330; *Testamenta Eboracensia*, 1:112, 4:213.

64. T. H. Turner, *Manners and Household Expenses of England* (London: Roxburghe Club, 1841), pp. 454–5.

65. François Béroalde de Verville, *Le Moyen de parvenir*, 3 vols (Paris: Léon Willem, 1870), 1:15.

66. James Raine (ed.), *Priory of Hexham*, 2 vols (Durham: Andrews and Co., 1864–5), 1:clxiv.

67. Michael Charles Burdet Dawes (ed.), *The Register of Edward the Black Prince*, 4 vols (London: His Majesty's Stationery Office, 1930–3), 4:68–71; *Testamenta Eboracensia*, 4:113–14.

68. See Malcolm H. Jones, 'Cats and Cat-skinning in Late Medieval Art and Life', in Sieglinde Hartmann (ed.), *Fauna and Flora in the Middle Ages: Studies of the Medieval Environment and Its Impact on the Human Mind* (Frankfurt: Peter Lang, 2007), pp. 97–112 (p. 98); Barbara Newman, 'The "Cattes Tale": A Chaucer Apocryphon', *Chaucer Review*, 26 (1992), 411–23.

69. John Lydgate, *Isopes Fabules*, 406, in Henry Noble MacCracken and Merriam Sherwood (eds), *The Minor Poems* 2 vols (London: Oxford University Press, 1911–34), 2:580; Robert Henryson, *Fables*, 326, in Denton Fox (ed.), *The Poems* (Oxford: Oxford University Press, 1981), p. 16; John Skelton, *Philip Sparrow*, 375,

in Gerald Hammond (ed.), *Selected Poems* (London: Routledge, 2003), p. 49.

70. 'A Talk of Ten Wives on Their Husbands' Ware', 26, in Eve Salisbury (ed.), *The Trials and Joys of Marriage* (Kalamazoo MI: Medieval Institute Publications, 2002), p. 99; Thomas Ravenscroft, 'Marriage of the Frogge and the Mouse', 37, in William Peacock (ed.), *English Verse: The Early Lyrics to Shakespeare* (London: Oxford University Press, 1928), p. 137; George Peele, *The Chronicle of King Edward the First, surnamed Longshanks*, ed. George Kelsey Dreher (Chicago IL: Adams Press, 1974), p. 15; Charles Whitworth (ed.), *Gammer Gurton's Needle* (London: Bloomsbury, 2012).

71. Edward Fairfax, *Daemonologia: A Discourse on Witchcraft*, ed. William Grainge (Harrogate: B. Ackrill, 1882), p. 33.

72. *Romaunt of the Rose*, C.6204–5, in *Riverside Chaucer*, p. 751; Paul D. A. Harvey and A. McGuinness, *A Guide to British Medieval Seals* (London: British Library, 1996), pp. 18, 90.

73. Bernard James Seubert (ed.), *Jeu saint Denis* (Geneva: Droz, 1974), p. 134; Laurence Bobis, *Une histoire du chat: de l'antiquité à nos jours* (Paris: Fayard, 2006), p. 68; Guillaume de Lorris and Jean de Meun, *Roman de la Rose*, 11068, ed. Ernest Langlois, 4 vols (Paris: Honoré Champion, 1914–23), 3:185; François Rabelais, *Œuvres complétes*, ed. Jacques Boulenger and Lucien Scheler (Paris: Librairie Gallimand, 1955), p. 219.

74. Kevin Murray (trans. and ed.), 'Catślechta and Other Medieval Legal Material Relating to Cats', *Celtica*, 25 (2007), 143–59 (pp. 146–9); Fergus Kelly, *Early Irish Farming: A Study Based Mainly on the Law-Texts of the 7th and 8th centuries AD* (Dublin: Institute for Advanced Studies, 1997), pp. 123–4.

75. Anthoni Smyters, *Het versierde woord. De Epitheta of woordcombinaties*, ed. Nicoline van der Sijs (Amsterdam: Het Taalfonds, 1999), p. 114; Georg Weitzenböck, 'Das Gefolge von lat. burra im Deutschen', *Zeitschrift für Mundartforschung*, 11 (1935), 204–31 (p. 219). See also Albert Hoefer, 'Deutsche Namen des Katers', *Germania*, 2 (1857), 168–71.

76. Kathleen Walker-Meikle, *Medieval Pets* (Woodbridge: Boydell, 2012), p. 71; Maximilian T. E. Seitz, 'Die Katze in der Sprache: Studien zur Etymologie, Semasiologie, Onomasiologie und Parömiologie' (unpublished PhD thesis, Ludwig Maximilian University of Munich, 1976), pp. 183–5.

77. Rabelais, *Œuvres complétes*, p. 727; William Baldwin, *Beware the Cat: The First English Novel*, ed. William A. Ringle⁻ and Michael Flachmann (San Marino CA: Huntington Library, 1988), pp. 11, 37.

78. Wilt L. Idema, *Mouse vs. Cat in Chinese Literature* (Seattle WA: University of Washington Press, 2019), pp. 42, 53–5; Museum of Fine Arts, Boston, accession no. 05.211. My thanks to Ms Mengge Wang for her help with these sources.

79. Joachim du Bellay, *Divers jeux rustiques*, ed. V. L. Saulnier (Geneva: Droz, 1965), pp. 104–10; Gerard Murphy (ed.), *Early Irish Lyrics: Eighth to Twelfth Century* (Dublin: Four Courts Press, 1998), pp. 2–4.

80. Gilles Ménage, *Dictionnaire étymologique* (Paris: Jean Anisson, 1694), p. 95; Anthony Emery, *Greater Medieval Houses of England and Wales, 1300–1500*, 3 vols (Cambridge: Cambridge University Press, 1996–2006), 3:487; William Tyndale, *Obedience of a Christian Man*, ed. David Daniell (London: Penguin, 2000), p. 83.

81. Ben Jonson, *Every Man Out of his Humour*, 4.5.122, ed. Helen Ostovich (Manchester: Manchester University Press, 2001), p. 314; Ben Parsons, 'Animal Names and the OED', *Notes and Queries*, 63/3 (2016), 370–4; Thomas III of Saluzzo, *Le livre du Chevalier errant*, ed. Robert Fajen (Wiesbaden: Reichert Verlag, 2019); Lyndsay, 'Testament and Complaynt of our Soverane Lordis Papyngo', in *Works*, 1:60–104.

82. See further Kathryn L. Smithies, *Introducing the Medieval Ass* (Cardiff: University of Wales Press, 2020), pp. 63–84.

83. Jan M. Ziolkowski, 'The Humour of Logic and the Logic of Humour in the Twelfth-Century Renaissance', *The Journal of Medieval Latin*, 3 (1993), 1–26 (pp. 24–5).

84. Nigellus Wireker, *Speculum Stultorum*, in Thomas Wright (ed.), *The Anglo-Latin Satirical Poets and Epigrammatists of the Twelfth Century*, 2 vols (London: Longman and Co., 1872), 1:3–145.

85. Paulus Venetus, *Logica Parva*, ed. Alan Perreiah (Leiden: Brill, 2002), p. 17; Henrici de Gandavo, *Quodlibet* X (Leiden: Brill, 1979), p. 57; Albert of Saxony, *Twenty-Five Disputed Questions on Logic*, ed. Michael J. Fitzgerald (Leiden: Brill, 2002), p. 290; C. Reinhard Hülsen, *Zur Semantik anaphorischer Pronomina Untersuchungen scholastischer und moderner Theorien* (Leiden: Brill, 1994), p. 183; Thomas Aquinis, *In libros Perihermenias, et posteriorum analyticorum* (Venice: Lucas Antonio Iunta, 1548), sig. Mm; Johannis Dolz Aragonensis, *Sillogismi* (Paris: Hemon le Freure, 1512), sig. C3.

86. R. M. Lumiansky and David Mills (eds), *Chester Mystery Cycle* (Oxford: Oxford University Press, 1974), p. 88; Chaucer, *Nun's Priest's Tale*, VII.3312, in *Riverside Chaucer*, p. 259.

87. Miguel de Cervantes, *El ingenioso hidalgo Don Quijote de la Mancha* (Madrid: Espasa-Calpe, 1960), p. 45.

88. Jill Mann (trans.), *Ysengrimus* (Leiden: Brill, 1987), p. 336; 'une figue aux parties honteuses de Tacor, et obligea tous les Milanois captifs d'arracher publiquement cette figue avec les dens ... à peine d'être pendus': Antoine Furetière, *Dictionnaire Universel, contenant généralement tous les mots*, 3 vols (The Hague: Arnout and Reinier Leers, 1690), 1:fol. Hhhh1v.

89. John Buridan, *Sophisms on Meaning and Truth*, trans. T. K. Scott (New York: Appleton-Century-Crofts, 1966), pp. 136–9. See further his *Summulae de dialectica* 4.3.8.4; *Quaestiones in Metaphysicam Aristotelis*, 7.16; *Quaestiones in Analytica Priora*, 2.19.1–3.

90. E. J. Ashworth, '"I Promise You a Horse": A Second Problem of Meaning and Reference in Late Fifteenth and Early Sixteenth Century Logic (I)', *Vivarium*, 14 (1976), 62–79.

91. See Michael Camille, 'Hybridity, Monstrosity and Bestiality in the Roman de Fauvel', in Marget Bent and Andrew Wathey (eds), *Fauvel Studies: Allegory, Chronicle, Music, and Image* (Oxford: Clarendon Press, 1993), pp. 165–71.

92. *Roman de la Rose*, 14037–75, 4:45–47; Larry D. Benson (ed.), *King Arthur's Death: The Middle English Stanzaic Morte Arthur and Alliterative Morte Arthure* (Idianapolis IN: Bobbs-Merril, 1975), p. 194.

93. 'De la dame qui aveinne demandoit pour Morel sa provande

avoir', in Willem Noomen and Nico van den Boogaard (eds), *Nouveau recueil complet des fabliaux*, 10 vols (Assen: Van Gorcum, 1983–98), 9:183–99.

94. 'Et diversis aliis nominibus appellant canes, deducentes etiam a patria nomen, ut Nato apud Britanos nomen est Britanus. Apud Gallos, Gallus, etc': Blondus, *De Canibus*, fol. 4v.

95. Robin S. Oggins, *The Kings and Their Hawks: Falconry in Medieval England* (New Haven CT: Yale University Press, 2004), p. 73.

96. Thomas Duffus Hardy (ed.), *Rotuli litterarum clausarum in Turri Londinensi asservati*, 2 vols (London: Records Commission, 1833–44), 1:192, 412; John MacLean (ed.), *Berkeley Manuscripts*, 3 vols (Gloucester: John Bellows, 1883–5), 2:363.

97. William Shakespeare, *The Tempest*, 4.1.254, in *Complete Works*, p. 1239; Thomas Nashe, *Summer's Last Will and Testament*, in J. B. Steane (ed.), *The Unfortunate Traveller and Other Works* (Harmondsworth: Penguin, 1972), p. 171; MacNab, 'Names', p. 365; Conradus Gesnerus, *Historiae Animalium Liber I de Quadrupedibus uiuiparis* (Zurich: Christopherus Froschoverum, 1551), p. 258.

98. Compare the list of birds permissible for different social groups appended to Juliana Berners, *The Boke of Saint Albans*, ed. William Blades (London: Elliot Stock, 1881), pp. 86–7

99. Edward Topsell, *The History of Four-Footed Beasts* (London: T. Muffet, 1658), p. 111.

100. *Sequel to the Adventures of Baron Munchausen* (London: H.D. Symonds, 1796), p. 46.

101. *Testamenta Eboracensia*, 2:249; F. Filippini, 'Inventario dei libri e dei beni posseduti add'arcivescoro di Ravenna Petrocino nel 1389', *Studi storici*, 6 (1897), 473–93 (p. 493).

102. William Langland, *Piers Plowman: The B-text*, 19.269–74, ed. A. V. C Schmidt (London: Dent, 1978), p. 243.

103. Magnús Magnússon and Hermann Pálsson (trans), *Laxdæla saga* (London: Folio Society, 1975), p. 106; Ben Parsons and Bas Jongenelen (trans. and eds), *Comic Drama in the Low Countries c.1450–1560* (Cambridge: D. S. Brewer, 2012), p. 78; Konrad von Megenberg, *Das "Buch der Natur": Bd. 2 – Kritischer Text nach den*

Handschriften, ed. Robert Luff and Georg Steer (Tübingen:
M. Niemeyer, 2003), p. 134.

104. Julia Boffey and A. S. G. Edwards, '"Chaucer's Chronicle", John
Shirley, and the Canon of Chaucer's Shorter Poems', *Studies in the
Age of Chaucer*, 20 (1998), 201–18 (pp. 217–8).

105. *Account of the Executors*, pp. 58–9.

106. H. D. Eshelby, 'Episcopal Visitations of the Yorkshire Deaneries
of the Archdeaconry of Richmond in 1548 and 1554', *Yorkshire
Archaeological Journal*, 14 (1898), 390–421 (p. 418).

107. John Mundy, 'Village, Town, and City in the Region of Toulouse',
in J. A. Raftis (ed.), *Pathways to Medieval Peasants* (Toronto:
Pontifical Institute, 1981), pp. 141–90 (pp. 188–9).

108. Marguerite Gonon, *La langue vulgaire écrite des testaments foréziens*
(Paris: Les Belles lettres, 1973), pp. 96, 122; Marguerite Gonon,
La vie familiale en Forez au XIVᵉ siècle (Paris: Les Belles lettres, 1961),
p. 216.

109. Chaucer, *Nun's Priest's Tale*, VII.2831 and *Prologue of the Wife of Bath*,
III.432, in *Riverside Chaucer*, pp. 253, 110; Laura Wright, *Sources
of London English: Medieval Thames Vocabulary* (Oxford: Clarendon
Press, 1996), p. 44.

110. Garrett P. J. Epps (ed.), *The Towneley Plays* (Kalamazoo MI:
Medieval Institute Press, 2017), p. 134; Erik Kooper (ed.),
Sentimental and Humorous Romances (Kalamazoo MI: Medieval
Institute Press, 2005), p. 190.

111. Thomas Harman, *A Caueat for Commen Cursetors* (London: Wylliam
Gryffith, 1567), sig. G3 (STC 12787).

112. Snorri Sturluson, *Gylfaginning*, ed. Gottfried Lorenz (Darmstadt:
Wissenschaftliche Buchgesellschaft, 1984), pp. 137–8; *Ragnars
saga loðbrókar*, in Guðni Jónsson and Bjarni Vilhjámsson (eds),
Fornaldarsögur Norðurlanda, 3 vols (Reykjavík: Bókaútgáfan Forni,
1943–4), 1:113; *Völuspá*, 41–2, in Dronke (ed.), *Poetic Edda*, 2:18.

113. Antoine Du Verdier, *La bibliotheque* (Lyon: Barthelemy Honorat,
1585), p. 188.

114. *Een batement vanden Preecker*, in W. N. M. Hüsken, B. A. M.
Ramakers and F. A. M. Schaars (eds), *Trou Moet Blijcken*.

Bronnenuitgave van de boeken der Haarlemse rederijkerskamer 'de Pellicanisten', 8 vols (Assen: Uitgeverij Quarto, 1992–8), 7:28.

115. *Ysengrimus*, 4.742–53, pp. 403–5.

116. 'Et parloit autant de lui comme |on fait| d'un larron de bois ou d'un cruel cappitaine, et disoit on aux gens qui alloient aux champs: "Gardez vous de Courtaut"': Alexandre Tuetey (ed.), *Journal d'un bourgeois de Paris 1405–1449: Publié d'après les manuscrits de Rome et de Paris* (Paris: H. Champion, 1881), pp. 348–9.

117. L. Bieler, 'Casconius, the Monster of the Navigatio Brendani', *Éigse*, 5 (1947), 139–40; R.C. Boer (ed.), *Qrvar-Odds Saga* (Leiden: Brill, 1888), p. 132; 'sē bið unwillum oft gemēted, frēcne and ferhðgrim, fareðlācendum, niþþa gehwylcum': Albert S. Cook (ed.), *The Old English Elene, Phœnix, and Physiologus* (New Haven CT: Yale University Press, 1919), p. 77.

118. Elizabeth Porges Watson, 'A Vulpine Martyr: The Fantasy of the Passion of the Fox', *Reinardus*, 6 (1993), 105–26. The name seems to echo the *Song*'s reference to 'Pharaoh's chariots' (*curribus Pharaonis*) (1.8), perhaps reinforced by its allusion to 'little foxes' (2.15).

119. Bernhard Walter Scholz and Barbara Rogers (trans.), *Carolingian Chronicles: Royal Frankish Annals and Nithard's Histories* (Ann Arbor MI: University of Michigan Press, 1970), p. 82

120. 'Uno elephante belissimo de anni zercha 6 … piangie come dona': Marino Sanudo, *I Diarii*, ed. F. Stefani et al., 58 vols (Venice: Spese Degli, 1879–1903), 18: col.59.

121. Stephan Oettermann, *Die Schaulust am Elefanten. Eine Elephantographia Curiosa* (Frankfurt: Syndikat, 1982), p. 110.

122. Somadeva, *Tales from the Kathāsaritsāgara*, trans. Arshia Sattar (London: Penguin, 1994), p. 114.

123. Abd al-Qadir Badayuni, *Muntakhab Ut-tawārikh*, trans. G. S. A. Ranking, W. H. Lowe and T. W. Haig, 3 vols (Kolkata: J.W. Thomas, 1884–1925), 2:98–99.

124. Badayuni, *Muntakhab Ut-tawārikh*, 2:243.

125. Wien Museum, Sammlung 76410 1.5.

126. Edmund Leach, 'Anthropological Aspects of Language', *The Essential Edward Leach* 1: *Anthropology and Society*, ed. Stephen Hugh-Jones and James Laidlaw (New Haven CT: Yale University Press, 2000), pp. 322–42 (pp. 323–4).

5.   IMPROPER NOUNS: HUMAN AND ANIMAL NAMES

1.   Philippe de Novare, *Mémoires: 1218–1243*, ed. by C. Kohler (Paris: H. Champion, 1913), p. 43.

2.   John Flinn, *Le Roman de Renart: Dans la littérature française et dans les littérature étrangères au Moyen Age* (Toronto: University of Toronto Press, 1963), pp. 159–71.

3.   R. Bossuat, *Le Roman de Renart* (Paris: Hatier-Bouvin, 1957), p. 151.

4.   Philippe de Novare, *Mémoires*, p. 44.

5.   'Phelippe de Nevaire avoit bien deviné et devisé en la branche de Renart ce que il firent aprés': Philippe de Novare, *Mémoires*, p. 51.

6.   'Cette branche dépasse … le cadre de la satire, elle est presque devenue un outil d'attaque individuelle': Naoyuki Fukumoto, 'Sur "une branche de Renart" par Philippe de Novare', *Miscellanea juslittera*, 1 (2016), 75–99 (p. 88).

7.   Claude Lévi-Strauss, *The Savage Mind*, trans. J. Weightman and D. Weightman (London: Weidenfield and Nicolson, 1966), p. 207.

8.   Robert Bartlett, *England Under the Norman and Angevin Kings* (Oxford: Clarendon, 2000), p. 668; Jeffrey Jerome Cohen, 'Inventing with Animals in the Middle Ages', in Alfred Kentigern Siewers (ed.), *Re-Imagining Nature* (Lanham MD: Bucknell University Press, 2014), pp. 141–58 (p. 142); Keith Thomas, *Man and the Natural World: Changing Attitudes in England 1500–1800* (London: Allen Lane, 1983), p. 114; Dorothy Yamamoto, *The Boundaries of the Human in Medieval English Literature* (Oxford: Oxford University Press, 2000), pp. 34–5.

9.   Stephen Wilson, *The Means of Naming* (London: Taylor and Francis, 1998), p. 240.

10. John MacLean (ed.), *Berkeley Manuscripts*, 3 vols (Gloucester: John Bellows, 1883–5), 2:363; John L'Estrange, 'Early Norfolk Wills from the Norfolk Registry', *Norfolk Antiquarian Miscellany*, 1 (1877), 345–412 (p. 392); *Wyl Bucke His Testament* (London: W. Copland, n.d.), STC 15118; F.W. Weaver, *Somerset Medieval Wills: 1501–1530* (London: Harrison and Sons, 1903), p. 230; Michael Charles Burdet Dawes (ed.), *The Register of Edward the Black Prince*, 4 vols (London: His Majesty's Stationery Office, 1930–3), 4:71.

11. 'Nous avons donne a un nombre infini d'animaux des noms d'hommes': Gilles Ménage, *Dictionnaire étymologique* (Paris: Jean Anisson, 1694), p. 489.

12. Malcolm Andrew (ed.), *Two Early Renaissance Bird Poems* (Washington DC: Folger, 1984), p. 62; John Lydgate, *Flour of Curtesye*, 58, in Kathleen Forni (ed.), *The Chaucerian Apocrypha* (Kalamazoo MI: Medieval Institute Press, 2005), p. 84.

13. John Conlee (ed.), *Middle English Debate Poetry: A Critical Anthology* (East Lansing MI: Colleagues Press, 1991), p. 289; Thomas Wright and Richard Paul Wülcker (eds), *Anglo-Saxon and Old English Vocabularies* (London: Trübner, 1884), p. 640; Thomas Elyot, *The Dictionary* (London: Thomas Berthelet, 1538), fol. 47 (STC 7659); A. P., *Natvral and morall questions* (London: Adam Islip, 1598), sig. F7 (STC 19054.5).

14. Thomas Hoccleve, 'Tale of Jonathas', 38, in Frederick J. Furnivall and I. Gollancz (eds) *The Minor Poems*, rev. Jerome Mitchell and A. I. Doyle (London: Oxford University Press, 1970), p. 217; Nicholas Love, *The Mirror of the Blessed Life of Jesus Christ*, ed. Michael G. Sargent (Exeter: University of Exeter Press, 2005), p. 152; Ranulph Higden, *Polychronicon*, trans. John Trevisa, ed. Churchill Babington and J. Rawson Lumby, 9 vols (London: Longman, 1865–86), 5:359.

15. John Florio, *A Worlde of Wordes* (London: Arnold Hatfield, 1598), p. 145 (STC 11098); *Fiue hundreth points of good husbandry* (London: Richard Tottel, 1573), fol. 45v (STC 24375); *Mar-Martine I know not why* (London: s.n., 1589), fol. 2 (STC 17461).

16. John Rastell, *Four Elements*, 414, in Richard Axton (ed.), *Three Rastell Plays* (Cambridge: Brewer, 1979), p. 405; Wendy Scase, *Piers Plowman and the New Anticlericalism* (Cambridge: Cambridge University Press, 1989), p. 171.

17. William Shakespeare, *Merchant of Venice*, 2.2.89, in *Complete Works*, gen. ed. Gary Taylor and Stanley Wells (Oxford: Oxford University Press, 2005), p. 460; John Humpheys, 'Transcript of the Estate Book of Robert Caldewell to John Talbot of Grafton Manor, Worcs., 1568–9', *Birmingham Archaeological Society Transactions*, 44 (1918), 15–124 (p. 67).

18. *Register of Edward*, 4:71; Peter Northeast and Heather Falvey (eds), *Wills of the Archdeaconry of Sudbury*, 1439–1474, 2 vols (Woodbridge: Boydell, 2001–10), 1:410.

19. J. Ernst Wülfing (ed.), *The Laud Troy Book*, 6506–7, 2 vols (London: K. Paul, Trench, Trübner, 1902–3), 1:192; F. J. Furnivall (ed.), *Fifty Earliest English Wills* (London: Oxford University Press, 1964), p. 53.

20. Fred Briggs, *An Index to Personal Names found in English Place-Names* (Nottingham: English Place-Name Society, 2021), p. 72.

21. W. G. Day (ed.), *The Pepys Ballads*, 5 vols (Cambridge: Brewer, 1987), 1:450; Thomas Churchyard, *Worthines of Wales* (London: Spenser Society, 1867), p. 57; *Strange and Horrible Cruelty of Elizabeth Stile* (London: John Allde, 1579), sig. D3 (STC 11537.5); *Examination, Confession, Triall, and Execution, of Joane Williford, Joan Cariden, and Jane Hott* (London: J. G., 1645), p. 1 (Wing E3712); Richard Bernard, *A Guide to Grand Iury-Men diuided into two bookes* (London: Felix Kingston, 1627), p. 187 (STC 1943).

22. Keith Briggs, 'The wolverine: an animal-name from a personal name?', *Journal of the English Place-Name Society*, 51 (2019), 69–70; Samuel Purchas, *Purchas his Pilgrimes*, 5 vols (London: William Stansby, 1625), 3:557 (STC 20506); John Jamieson, *Etymological Dictionary of the Scottish Language*, 4 vols (Edinburgh: Edinburgh University Press, 1808–41), 4:683.

23. For additional examples, see Ben Parsons, 'Pet Names and the OED', *Notes and Queries* 63/3 (2016), 370–4.

24. Geoffrey Chaucer, *General Prologue*, l.643, in *Riverside Chaucer*, gen. ed. Larry D. Benson (Oxford: Oxford University Press, 2008), p. 33.

25. *Middle English Debate Poetry*, p. 289; John Gower *Vox Clamantis*, 1.9, in G. C. Macauley (ed.), *Complete Works: The Latin Works* (Oxford: Clarendon Press, 1902), pp. 44–5.

26. Celia Sisam and Kenneth Sisam (eds), *The Oxford Book of Medieval English Verse* (Oxford: Clarendon, 1970), pp. 413–21.

27. *The Complaynte of them that ben to late maryed*, 314, in A. E. B. Coldiron (ed.), *English Printing, Verse Translation. and the Battle of the Sexes, 1476–1557* (Farnham: Ashgate, 2009), p. 223; 'The Schoolboy's Lament', in Derek Pearsall (ed.), *From Chaucer to Spenser* (Oxford: Blackwell, 2009), p. 399.

28. Alan Crossley, *Oxford City Apprentices* (Oxford: Clarendon Press, 2012), p. 123; John Rider, *Bibliotheca scholastica* (Oxford: Joseph Barnes, 1589), col. 684 (STC 21031.5).

29. William Shakespeare, *Merry Wives of Windsor*, 2.3.57, 3.1.77, in *Complete Works*, pp. 522–3; Thomas Nashe, *Lenten Stuff*, in J. B. Steane (ed.), *The Unfortunate Traveller and Other Works* (Harmondsworth: Penguin, 1972), p. 453; Thomas Killigrew, *The Parson's Wedding*, 3.2, in Alexander Norman Jeffares (ed.), *Restoration Comedy* (London: Folio Press, 1974), p. 62; Francis Willughby, *Ornithologiae*, 3 vols (London: John Martyn, 1676), pp. 214–5; Richard Blome, *Gentlemans Recreation*, 2 vols (London: Richard Blome, 1686), 2:28, 2:91–2 (Wing B3213); Alex. Old., 'To his Ingenious Friend the Translator', in Carlo Moscheni, *Brutes Turn'd Criticks, or, Mankind Moraliz'd by Beasts*, trans. John Savage (London: Daniel Dring, 1695), sig. A12 (Wing M2851).

30. Alastair Fowler (ed.), *The Country House Poem: A Cabinet of Seventeenth-Century Estate Poems and Related Items* (Edinburgh: Edinburgh University Press, 1994), 208–15: Willughby, *Ornithologiae*, p. 18.

31. Ménage, *Dictionnaire étymologique*, pp. 571, 489, 477.

32. Jacques Derrida, *The Animal That Therefore I Am* trans. David Wills, ed. Marie-Louise Mallet (New York: Fordham University Press,

2008), pp. 9, 34. See also Carolynn van Dyke, 'Naming of the Beasts: Tracking the *Animot* in Medieval Texts', *Studies in the Age of Chaucer*, 34 (2012), 1–51 (pp. 32–4).

33. Thomas Wright and James Orchard Halliwell (eds), *Reliquæ Antiquæ*, 2 vols (London: John Russell Smith, 1841–3), 1:133.

34. Bodleian Library, MS Digby 86, fol. 168–8v.

35. Donald A. Ringe, *From Proto-Indo-European to Proto-Germanic* (Oxford: Oxford University Press, 2017), p. 128; Keith Allan and Kate Burridge, *Forbidden Words: Taboo and the Censoring of Language* (Cambridge: Cambridge University Press, 2002), p. 39.

36. Franz Steiner, *Taboo* (Harmondsworth: Pelican, 1967), pp. 20–1.

37. Warren Ginsburg (ed.), *Wynnere and Wastoure and the Parlement of Thre Ages* (Kalamazoo MI: Medieval Institute Publications, 1992), p. 13; Ranulph Higden, *Polychronicon*, trans. John Trevisa, ed. Charles Babington and J. Rawson Lumby, 9 vols (London: Longman, 1865–86), 1:359.

38. Richard Kieckhefer (trans. and ed.), *Hazards of the Dark Arts* (University Park PA: Pennsylvania University Press, 2017), p. 60; Paul Hamelius (ed.), *Mandeville's Travels: The Cotton Version* (London: K. Paul, Trench, Trübner and Co., 1919–23), 1:110.

39. Andrew Boorde, *Dyetary of Helth* (London: Robert Wyer, n.d.), sig. I2 (STC 3378.5); Robert Burton, *The Anatomy of Melancholy*, ed. Holbrook Jackson (New York: Vintage Books, 1977), p. 138. Early witnesses to the hare's seasonal madness include John Skelton, *The Book of the Laurel*, ed. F.W. Brownlow (Cranbury NJ: Associated University Presses, 1990), p. 126; Thomas More, 'Supplication of Souls', in Frank Manley et al. (eds), *Complete Works*, 15 vols (New Haven CT: Yale University Press, 1990), 7:137; John Heywood, A *Dialogue of Proverbs*, ed. Rudolph E. Habenicht (Berkeley CA: University of California Press, 1963), p. 154; 'Colyn Blowbols Testament', in W. Carew Hazlitt (ed.), *Remains of the Early Popular Poetry of England*, 4 vols (London: John Russell Smith, 1864–6), 1:105.

40. Robert Wodrow, *Analecta: Or Materials for a History of Remarkable Providences*, 4 vols (London: Maitland Club, 1842), 2:62.

41. Madeleine Jeay and Kathleen Garay (trans. and eds), *The Distaff Gospels* (Peterborough ON: Broadview, 2006), p. 107; Juliana Berners, *The Book of Saint Albans* (New York: Abercrombie and Fitch, 1966), p. 123; John Hodgkin, 'Proper Terms: An Attempt at a Rational Explanation of the Meanings of the Collection of Phrases in "The Book of St Albans"', *Transactions of the Philological Society*, 1907–10 (London: Kegan Paul, 1910), pp. 1–187 (p. 33).

42. William Shakespeare, *Macbeth*, 3.4.124–6, in *Complete Works*, p. 983; Tiziana Frati, *Bruegel: The Complete Paintings*, trans. Jane Carroll (London: Granada, 1980), p. 80.

43. Radulphe Gualthere, *An hundred, threescore and fiftene homelyes or sermons*, trans. John Bridges (London: Henrie Denham, 1572), p. 866 (STC 25013); W. H. D. Rouse, 'Tokens of death', *Folk-Lore*, 4 (1893), 258.

44. Mariko Miyazaki, 'Misericord Owls and Medieval Anti-semitism', in Debra Hassig (ed.), *The Mark of the Beast: The Medieval Bestiary in Art, Life, and Literature* (New York: Garland, 1999), pp. 23–49 (p. 36).

45. 'Report on Dorset Natural History for 1951', *Proceedings of the Dorset Natural History and Archaeological Society*, 73–5 (1951), 172; J. G. Frazer, *The Golden Bough*, 12 vols (London: Macmillan, 1906–15), 3:233.

46. William Shakespeare, *Two Gentlemen of Verona*, 2.3.6, in *Complete Works*, p. 8.

47. Michaele Angelus Blondus, *De Canibus et venatione* (Rome: Antonius Bladus Asulanus, 1544), fol. 4v; Willem Ockers, *Amsterdams Honden-Mirakel* (Rotterdam, etc.: Wed. Vis et al., c.1766), pp. 17–18.

48. University of Leeds, Brotherton Collection MS Lt q 22. My thanks to Dr Rosamund Paice and Prof Mary Ann Lund for bringing this source to my attention.

49. Theodore Zeldin, *An Intimate History of Humanity* (London: Minerva, 1995), p. 137.

50. Charles Wareing Bardsley, *Curiosities of Puritan Nomenclature* (London: Chatto and Windus, 1888), p. 6; Tauno F. Mustanoja,

'The Suggestive Use of Christian Names in Middle English Poetry', in Jerome Mandel and Bruce A. Rosenberg (eds), *Medieval Literature and Folklore Studies: Essays in Honor of Francis Lee Utley* (New Brunswick NJ: Rutgers University Press, 1970), pp. 51–76 (p. 57); Emily Steiner, 'Naming and Allegory in Late Medieval England', *Journal of English and Germanic Philology*, 106 (2007), 248–75 (p. 268).

51. 'A Lutel Soth Sermun', in Richard Morris (ed.), *An Old English Miscellany* (London: N. Trübner and Co., 1872), pp. 187–91; 'Satire on the Consistory Courts', in Rossell Hope Robbins (ed.), *Historical Poems of the XIVth and XVth Centuries* (London: Oxford University Press, 1959), pp. 24–7.

52. William Langland, *Piers Plowman: The B-text*, 5.309–23, ed. A. V. C. Schmidt (London: Dent, 1978), p. 53.

53. Ranulph Higden, *Polychronicon*, ed. Joseph Rawson Rumby, 9 vols (London: Longman, 1865–86), 8:455; 'Versus de tempore Johannis Straw', in Thomas Wright (ed.), *Political Poems and Songs*, 2 vols (London: Longman, 1859), 1:230.

54. 'The Shepherds (2)', in Garrett P. J. Epps (ed.), *The Towneley Plays* (Kalamazoo MI: Medieval Institute Press, 2017), p. 132.

55. Conradus Gesnerus, *Historiae Animalium Liber I de Quadrupedibus uiuiparis* (Zurich: Christopherus Froschoverum, 1551), p. 218; Karl Rygh, *Norske og islandiske tilnavne fra oldtiden og middelalderen* (s.l.: s.n., 1800), p. 61.

56. Hans Wanner, 'Hundenamen aus dem Anfang des 16. Jahrhunderts', in Karl Friedrich Müller (ed.), *Beiträge zur Sprachwissenschaft und Volkskunde* (Lahr: Moritz Schauenburg, 1951), pp. 219–23 (pp. 220–1).

57. Thomas Duffus Hardy (ed.), *Rotuli litterarum clausarum in Turri Londinensi asservati*, 2 vols (London: Records Commission, 1833–44), 1:412.

58. *Moorkens-vel vande quade wijuen*, in *Veelderhande geneuchlijcke dichten, tafelspelen ende refereynen* (Utrecht: H. E. S. Publishers, 1977), pp. 21–39; *Register of Edward*, 4:113–4.

59. Marcelo E. Fuentes, *Contradictory Muslims in the Literature of*

Medieval Iberian Christians (London: Palgrave MacMillan, 2023), pp. 25–7.

60. Albert Memmi, *Racism* (Minneapolis MN: University of Minnesota Press, 2000); Richard Dyer, *White: Essays on Race and Culture* (London: Routledge, 1997), pp. 1–40.

61. François Raymond, *Dictionnaire général de la langue française*, 2 vols (Paris: Aimé André, 1842), 2:698.

62. Geraldine Heng, *The Invention of Race in the European Middle Ages* (Cambridge: Cambridge University Press, 2018), pp. 181–256.

63. 'Abuses of Names', *Universal Magazine*, January 1768, p. 40.

64. James Woodforde, *Diary of a Country Parson, 1758–1802*, ed. John Beresford (Oxford: Oxford University Press, 1978), p. 136; *Trewman's Exeter Flying Post*, 7 January 1819, p. 1; Mrs Sherwood, *The Little Woodman and his Dog Caesar* (Wellington: F. Houlston and Son, 1818); Nat Nimrod, 'A Sporting General's Despatches', *Sporting Magazine*, April 1794, p. 16.

65. Alan J. Rice, *Radical Narratives of the Black Atlantic* (London: Continuum, 2003), p. 211.

66. Samuel Birch, *Book of Negros*, National Archives, Kew, PRO 30/55/100.

67. Aphra Behn, *Oroonoko, and Other Works*, ed. Paul Salzman (Oxford: Oxford University Press, 1998), p. 39.

68. John Block Friedman, *The Monstrous Races in Medieval Art and Thought* (Cambridge MA: Harvard University Press, 1981), pp. 178–96; Debra Higgs Strickland, *Saracens, Demons, and Jews: Making Monsters in Medieval Art* (Princeton NJ: Princeton University Press, 2003).

69. Gonzalo Fernández de Oviedo, *Historia general y natural de las Indias*, ed. José Amador de los Ríos, 4 vols (Madrid: Real Academia de la Historia, 1851–3), 2:3.

70. Paul H. Freedman, *Images of the Medieval Peasant* (Stanford CA: Stanford University Press, 1999), p. 140.

71. Giorgio Agamben, *The Open: Man and Animal*, trans. Kevin Attell (Stanford CA: Stanford University Press, 2004), p. 24.

72. Derrida, *The Animal That Therefore I Am*, pp. 34, 104.

6.   FINAL CALL: CONCLUSIONS

1.   Samuel Beckett, *Collected Shorter Plays* (London: Faber and Faber, 1984), p. 35.

2.   Susan McHugh, Robert McKay and John Miller, 'Towards an Animal-Centred Literary History', in Susan McHugh, Robert McKay and John Miller (eds), *Palgrave Handbook of Animals and Literature* (London: Palgrave, 2020), pp. 1–11 (p. 9).

3.   R. W. Connell, *Masculinities* (Cambridge: Polity, 2005), p. 81.

4.   'Dominus enim creaturas creauit diuersas naturas habentes, non solum ad sustentationem hominum, sed etiam ad doctrinam eorum, ut per ipsas creaturas non solum inspiciamus quid nobis utile sit in corpora, sed etiam quid sit utile in anima': Thomas de Chobham, *Summa de arte praedicandi*, ed. Franco Morenzoni (Turnhout: Brepols, 1988), p. 275.

5.   Jacques Derrida, *The Animal That Therefore I Am*, trans. David Wills, ed. Marie-Louise Mallet (New York: Fordham University Press, 2008), p. 25.

6.   Kate Ng, 'These are the most popular pet names of 2022', *The Independent*, 10 October 2022.

7.   Caroline Bressey, 'It's Only Political Correctness – Race and Racism in British History', in Caroline Bressey and Claire Dwyer (eds), *New Geographies of Race and Racism* (London: Routledge, 2008), pp. 29–39.

8.   Robert D. Sack, 'The Inadequacy of Human-Nature Theory and the View of Mass Consumption', in B. L. Turner et al. (ed.), *The Earth as Transformed by Human Action* (Cambridge: Cambridge University Press, 1990), pp. 659–72 (p. 669).

9.   Peter Singer, *Animal Liberation* (London: Pimlico, 1995), p. 95.

SELECT
BIBLIOGRAPHY

Agamben, Giorgio, *The Open: Man and Animal*, trans. Kevin Attell (Stanford CA: Stanford University Press, 2004).

Badayuni, Abd al-Qadir, *Muntak̲h̲ab Ut-tawārik̲h̲*, trans. G. S. A. Ranking, W. H. Lowe and T. W. Haig, 3 vols (Kolkata: J. W. Thomas, 1884–1925).

Baldwin, William, *Beware the Cat: The First English Novel*, ed. William A. Ringler and Michael Flachmann (San Marino CA: Huntington Library, 1988).

Baratay, Éric (ed.), *Aux sources de l'histoire animale* (Paris: Éditions de la Sorbonne, 2019).

Barber, Richard, *Bestiary: Being an English Version of the Bodleian Library, Oxford MS Bodley 764* (Woodbridge: Boydell, 1993).

Bartlett, Robert, *England Under the Norman and Angevin Kings* (Oxford: Clarendon, 2000).

Bentham, Jeremy, *Chrestomathia*, ed. M. J. Smith and W. H. Burston (Oxford: Clarendon Press, 1983).

Bernard, Richard, *A Guide to Grand Iury-Men* (London: Felix Kingston, 1627), STC 1943.

Bieler, L., 'Casconius, the Monster of the Navigatio Brendani', *Ēigse*, 5 (1947), 139–40.

Bliss, Jane, *Naming and Namelessness in Medieval Romance* (Woodbridge: Boydell, 2008).

Blome, Richard, *Gentlemans Recreation*, 2 vols (London: Richard Blome, 1686), Wing B3213.

Blondus, Michaele Angelus, *De Canibus et venatione* (Rome: Antonius Bladus Asulanus, 1544).

Boehrer, Bruce Thomas, Molly Hand and Brian Massumi (eds), *Animals, Animality, and Literature* (Cambridge: Cambridge University Press, 2018).

Bowers, John M. (ed.), *The Canterbury Tales: Fifteenth-Century Continuations and Additions* (Kalamazoo MI: Medieval Institute Publications, 1992)

Breasted, James Henry, *Ancient Records of Egypt III: The Nineteenth Dynasty* (Chicago IL: University of Chicago Press, 1906).

Briggs, Keith, 'The wolverine: an animal-name from a personal name?', *Journal of the English Place-Name Society*, 51 (2019), 69–70.

Briggs, Keith, *An Index to Personal Names found in English Place-Names* (Nottingham: English Place-Name Society, 2021).

Castets, Ferdinand (ed.), *Quatre Fils Aymon* (Geneva: Slatkine, 1974).

Chadwick, John, J. T. Killen and J.-P. Oliver, *The Knossos Tablets* (Cambridge: Cambridge University Press, 1971).

Chaucer, Geoffrey, *Riverside Chaucer*, gen. ed. Larry D. Benson (Oxford: Oxford University Press, 2008).

Clutton-Brock, Juliet, *Animals as Domesticates: A World View through History* (East Lansing MI: Michigan State University Press, 2012).

Cohen, Jeffrey Jerome, 'Inventing with Animals in the Middle Ages', in Alfred Kentigern Siewers (ed.), *Re-Imagining Nature* (Lanham MD: Bucknell University Press, 2014), pp. 141–58.

Conlee, John W. (ed.), *Middle English Debate Poetry* (East Lansing MI: Colleagues Press, 1991).

Crane, Susan, *Animal Encounters: Contacts and Concepts in Medieval Britain* (Pittsburgh PA: University of Pennsylvania Press, 2012).

Davis, Norman, Richard Beadle and Colin Richmond (eds), *Paston*

Letters and Papers of the Fifteenth Century, 3 vols (Oxford: Clarendon Press, 2004–5).

Dawes, Michael Charles Burdet (ed.), *The Register of Edward the Black Prince*, 4 vols (London: His Majesty's Stationery Office, 1930–3).

de Brézé, Jacques, *La Chasse, les Dits du bon chien Souillard et les Louanges de Madame Anne de France*, ed. Gunnar Tilander (Lund: Bloms, 1959).

de Lorris, Guillaume, and Jean de Meun, *Roman de la Rose*, 11068, ed. Ernest Langlois, 4 vols (Paris: Honoré Champion, 1914–23).

de Oviedo, Gonzalo Fernández, *Historia general y natural de las Indias*, ed. José Amador de los Ríos, 4 vols (Madrid: Real Academia de la Historia, 1851–3).

Derrida, Jacques, *The Animal That Therefore I Am*, trans. David Wills, ed. Marie-Louise Mallet (New York: Fordham University Press, 2008).

Dronke, Ursula (ed.), *Poetic Edda*, 3 vols (Oxford: Oxford University Press, 1969–2011).

Duchet-Suchaux, Gaston, 'Le nom des animaux au Moyen Âge', *Actes des colloques de la Société française d'onomastique*, 12 (2004), 87–90.

Duggan, Joseph J., and Karen Akiyama (ed.), *La Chanson de Roland*, 2 vols (Turnhout: Brepols, 2005).

Epp, Garrett P. J. (ed.), *The Towneley Plays* (Kalamazoo MI: Medieval Institute Publications, 2017).

Evans, E. P., *The Criminal Prosecution and Capital Punishment of Animals* (London: William Heinemann, 1906).

Gantz, Jeffrey (trans.), *The Mabinogion* (Harmondsworth: Penguin, 1976).

Gautier, Léon, *La Chevalerie* (Paris: Victor Palmé, 1884).

Gesnerus, Conradus, *Historiae Animalium Liber I de Quadrupedibus uiuiparis* (Zurich: Christopherus Froschoverum, 1551).

Gonon, Marguerite, *La langue vulgaire écrite des testaments foréziens* (Paris: Les Belles lettres, 1973).

Gonon, Marguerite, *La vie familiale en Forez au XIVe siècle* (Paris: Les Belles lettres, 1961).

Gower, John, *Complete Works: The Latin Works*, G. C. Macauley (Oxford: Oxford University Press, 1902).

Hale, William, and H. T. Ellacombe (eds), *Account of the Executors of Richard Bishop of London* (London: Camden Society, 1874).

Hardy, Thomas Duffus (ed.), *Rotuli litterarum clausarum in Turri Londinensi asservati*, 2 vols (London: Records Commission, 1833–44).

Higden, Ranulf, *Polychronicon*, trans. John Trevisa, ed. Charles Babington and J. Rawson Lumby, 9 vols (London: Longman, 1865–86).

Hoefer, Albert, 'Deutsche Namen des Katers', *Germania*, 2 (1857), 168–71.

Homer, *Iliad*, trans. and ed. A. T. Murray and William F. Wyatt, 2 vols (Cambridge MA: Harvard University Press, 1999).

Hüsken, W. N. M., B. A. M. Ramakers and F. A. M. Schaars (eds), *Trou Moet Blijcken. Bronnenuitgave van de boeken der Haarlemse rederijkerskamer 'de Pellicanisten'*, 8 vols (Assen: Uitgeverij Quarto, 1992–8).

Hyginus, *Fabulae*, ed. P. K. Marshall (Stuttgart: B. G. Teubner Verlagsgesellschaft, 1993).

Isidorus Hispalensis, *Etymologiae sive originum*, 12.2.25–6, ed. W. M Lindsay, 2 vols (Oxford: Clarendon Press, 1911).

Jamieson, John, *Etymological Dictionary of the Scottish Language*, 4 vols (Edinburgh: Edinburgh University Press, 1808–41).

Jones, Malcom H., *The Secret Middle Ages* (Stroud: Sutton, 2002).

Kripke, Saul A., *Naming and Necessity* (Cambridge MA: Harvard University Press, 1980).

Langland, William, *Piers Plowman: The B-text*, ed. A. V. C. Schmidt (London: Dent, 1978).

Leach, Edmund, *The Essential Edward Leach 1: Anthropology and Society*, ed. Stephen Hugh-Jones and James Laidlaw (New Haven CT: Yale University Press, 2000).

Leibring, Katharina, 'Animal Names', in Carole Hough (ed.), Oxford *Handbook of Names and Naming* (Oxford: Oxford University Press, 2016), pp. 615–27.

Lemaire de Belges, Jean, *Les épîtres de l'amant vert*, ed. Jean Frappier (Geneva: Droz, 1948).

Lévi-Strauss, Claude, *The Savage Mind*, trans. J. Weightman and D. Weightman (London: Weidenfield and Nicolson, 1966).

Lewis, Sîan, and Lloyd Llewellyn-Jones, *The Culture of Animals in Antiquity* (London: Routledge, 2018).

Librova, Bohdana, 'Quelques observations sur les emplois figurés des noms du chien en français médiéval', in Dora Faraci (ed.), *Simbolismo animale e letteratura* (Manziana: Vecchiarelli, 2003), pp. 61–88.

Lovejoy, Arthur O., *The Great Chain of Being: A Study of the History of an Idea* (Cambridge MA: Harvard University Press, 1936).

Lyndsay, David, *Poetical Works*, ed. David Laing (Edinburgh: William Patterson, 1871).

MacGregor, Lesley Bates, 'Criminalising Animals in Medieval France', *Open Library of Humanities*, 5 (2019).

Mann, Jill (trans.), *Ysengrimus* (Leiden: Brill, 1987).

Marvin, Corey J., *Word Outward: Medieval Perspectives on the Entry into Language* (New York: Routledge, 2001).

McHugh, Susan, Robert McKay and John Miller (eds), Palgrave *Handbook of Animals and Literature* (London: Palgrave, 2020).

McLure, Peter, 'Interpretation of Hypocoristic Forms of Middle English Baptismal Names', *Nomina*, 21 (1998), 103.

Ménage, Gilles, *Dictionnaire étymologique* (Paris: Jean Anisson, 1694).

Mommsen, Theodor, et al., *Corpus Inscriptionum Latinarum*, 17 vols (Berlin: Georgius Reimerus; Deutsche Akademie der Wissenschaften zu Berlin, 1871–2015).

Murray, Kevin (trans. and ed.), 'Catslechta and Other Medieval Legal Material Relating to Cats', *Celtica*, 25 (2007), 143–59.

Mustanoja, Tauno F., 'The Suggestive Use of Christian Names in Middle English Poetry', in Jerome Mandel and Bruce A. Rosenberg (eds), *Medieval Literature and Folklore Studies: Essays in Honor of Francis Lee Utley* (New Brunswick NJ: Rutgers University Press, 1970), pp. 51–76.

Nashe, Thomas, *The Unfortunate Traveller and Other Works*, ed. J. B. Steane (Harmondsworth: Penguin, 1972).

Noomen, Willem, and Nico van den Boogaard (eds), *Nouveau recueil complet des fabliaux*, 10 vols (Assen: Van Gorcum, 1983–98).

Northeast, Peter, and Heather Falvey (eds), *Wills of the Archdeaconry of Sudbury, 1439–1474*, 2 vols (Woodbridge: Boydell, 2001–10).

Oesterley, Hermann (ed.), *Gesta Romanorum*, 2 vols (Berlin: Weidmann-sche Buchhandlung, 1872).

Oggins, Robin S., *The Kings and Their Hawks: Falconry in Medieval England* (New Haven CT: Yale University Press, 2004).

Ovid, *Metamorphoses*, ed. Frank Justus Miller and G. P. Goold, 2 vols (Cambridge MA: Harvard University Press, 1977).

Ovid, *Metamorphoses*, trans. Arthur Golding, ed. John Frederick Nims (Philadelphia PA: Paul Dry, 2000).

Ovid, *Metamorphosis Englished*, trans. George Sandys (London: William Stansby, 1626), STC 18964.

Parsons, Ben, 'Pet Names and the OED', *Notes and Queries*, 63/3 (2016), 370–4.

Paton, W. R. (ed.), *Greek Anthology*, 5 vols (Cambridge MA: Harvard University Press, 1914–18).

Plutarch, *Moralia*, trans. and ed. Frank Cole Babbitt, 15 vols (Cambridge MA: Harvard University Press, 1936).

Procopius, *History of the Wars*, trans. and ed. H. R. Dewing, 5 vols (Cambridge MA: Harvard University Press, 1935).

Rabelais, François, *Œuvres complétes*, ed. Jacques Boulenger and Lucien Scheler (Paris: Librairie Gallimand, 1955).

Raine, James, et al. (eds), *Testamenta Eboracensia*, 6 vols (London: J. B. Nichols, 1836–1902).

Ribémont, Bernard, 'Histoires de perroquets: petit itinéraire zoologique et poétique', *Reinardus*, 8/3 (1990), 155–71.

Room, Adrian, *The Naming of Animals* (Jefferson, NC: McFarland, 1993).

Salisbury, Joyce E., *The Beast Within: Animals in the Middle Ages* (Abingdon: Routledge, 2011).

Scott-Macnab, David, 'The Names of All Manner of Hounds:

A Unique Inventory in a Fifteenth-Century Manuscript', *Viator*, 44 (2013), 339–68.

Serpell, James A., 'Guardian Spirits or Demonic Pets: The Concept of the Witch's Familiar in Early Modern England, 1530–1712', in A. N. H. Creager and W. C. Jordan (eds), *The Human/Animal Boundary* (Cambridge: Cambridge University Press, 1996), pp. 157–90.

Shakespeare, William, *Complete Works*, gen. ed. Gary Taylor and Stanley Wells (Oxford: Oxford University Press, 2005).

Sharpe, Reginald R. (ed.), *Calendar of Wills Proved and Enrolled in the Court of Hustings*, 2 vols (London: John C. Francis, 1889–90).

Singer, Peter, *Animal Liberation* (London: Pimlico, 1995).

Smithies, Kathryn L., *Introducing the Medieval Ass* (Cardiff: University of Wales Press, 2020).

Steiner, Emily, 'Naming and Allegory in Late Medieval England', *Journal of English and Germanic Philology*, 106 (2007), 248–75.

McHugh, Susan, Robert McKay and John Miller (eds), Palgrave *Handbook of Animals and Literature* (London: Palgrave, 2020).

Thomas, Keith, *Man and the Natural World: Changing Attitudes in England* 1500–1800 (London: Allen Lane, 1983).

Tolkien, J. R. R., E. V. Gordon and Norman Davis (eds), *Sir Gawain and the Green Knight* (Oxford: Oxford University Press, 1967).

Toynbee, J. M. C., 'Beasts and their Names in the Roman Empire', *Papers of the British School at Rome*, 16 (1948), 24–37.

Toynbee, J. M. C., *Animals in Roman Life and Art* (Ithaca NY: Cornell University Press, 1973).

Unger, Carl Rikard (ed.), *Saga Điðriks konungs af Bern* (Copenhagen: Feilberg and Landmarks Forlag, 1853).

Van Dyke, Carolynn, 'Naming of the Beasts: Tracking the Animot in Medieval Texts', *Studies in the Age of Chaucer*, 34 (2012), 1–51.

Walker-Meikle, Kathleen, 'Late Medieval Pet-Keeping' (unpublished PhD thesis, University College London, 2013).

Walker-Meikle, Kathleen, *Medieval Pets* (Cambridge: Boydell and Brewer, 2012).

Wanner, Hans, 'Hundenamen aus dem Anfang des 16. Jahrhunderts', in Karl Friedrich Müller (ed.), *Beiträge zur Sprachwissenschaft und Volkskund* (Lahr: Moritz Schauenburg, 1951), pp. 219–23.

Watson, Elizabeth Porges, 'A Vulpine Martyr: The Fantasy of the Passion of the Fox', *Reinardus*, 6/1 (1993), 105–26.

Wilkins, John S., *Species: A History of the Idea* (Berkeley CA: University of California Press, 2009).

Wilson, Stephen, *The Means of Naming* (London: Taylor and Francis, 1998).

Wireker, Nigellus, *Speculum Stultorum*, in Thomas Wright (ed.), *The Anglo-Latin Satirical Poets and Epigrammatists of the Twelfth Century*, 2 vols (London: Longman and Co., 1872).

Wolfe, Cary, 'Human, All Too Human: "Animal Studies" and the Humanities', *Publications of the Modern Language Association of America*, 124 (2009), 564–76.

Wolfe, Cary, *Animal Rites: American Culture, the Discourse of Species, and Posthumanist Theory* (Chicago IL: University of Chicago Press, 2003).

Xenophon, *Scripta minora*, trans. and ed. E. C. Marchant and G. W. Bowersock (Cambridge MA: Harvard University Press, 1968).

Yamamoto, Dorothy, *The Boundaries of the Human in Medieval English Literature* (Oxford: Oxford University Press, 2000).

Zatta, Claudia, *Aristotle and the Animals: The Logos of Life Itself* (Abingdon: Routledge, 2022).

Zeldin, Theodore, *An Intimate History of Humanity* (London: Minerva, 1995).

Ziolkowski, Jan M., *Talking Animals: Medieval Latin Beast Poetry, 75–1150* (Philadelphia PA: University of Pennsylvania Press, 1993).

INDEX